CHARMED BEGINNINGS

A beginner's guide to patchwork and quilting

Jo Baddeley

PUDDLEDUCKS PUBLICATIONS

Charmed Beginnings

First published in 2010 by Teamwork Craftbooks
under the imprint 'Puddleducks Publications'

Puddleducks, 116 St John's Hill, Sevenoaks, Kent, TN13 3PD
www.puddleducksquilts.co.uk

Text, photographs and quilt designs © Jo Baddeley
(apart from *Floating Flower Charms*, design © Mimi Hollenbaugh)

Illustrations © Gail Lawther

The designs, illustrations and other material in this book may not be used for workshops
without obtaining prior permission (in writing) from the author.
These designs may not be stitched for resale.

The right of Jo Baddeley to be identified as the Author of this Work has been asserted
by her in accordance with the Copyright, Designs and Patents Act 1988.

All rights reserved. No part of this publication may be reproduced, stored in a retrieval system,
or transmitted in any form or by any means, electronic, mechanical, photocopying, recording or otherwise,
without the prior permission of the publisher or a licence permitting restricted copying.

The use of trade names in this book is in no way intended to be an infringement of copyright.
The author, the publishers and their representatives can accept no legal responsibility
for any consequence arising from the application of information, advice or instructions
given in this book.

ISBN 978 0 9553499 4 2

British Library Cataloguing in Publication Data
A catalogue record for this book is available from the British Library

Designed by Teamwork: Christopher & Gail Lawther
100 Wiston Avenue, Worthing, West Sussex, BN14 7PS
e-mail: thelawthers@ntlworld.com

Set in ITC Goudy Sans & Myriad

Printed by Kenads, Goring-by-Sea, West Sussex
www.kenadsprinters.co.uk

Introduction

If you are a beginner – welcome to the world of patchwork and quilting! If you have done patchwork before, I hope you will find that this book inspires you to use some of the wonderful prints on the market in simple, but stunning, quilt projects.

My addiction to fabric started in childhood – pretty Liberty-lawn smocked dresses led onto those oh-so-psychedelic 70s prints. Like many quilters, I too have an (unfinished) hexagon quilt – made from all those memorable fabrics – in the loft, still tacked to the paper templates. But the craft of patchwork and quilting has been transformed in recent years with the development of new tools such as the rotary cutter and ruler, through to commercial long-arm quilting machines – and now you really can make a quilt in hours rather than months. Fabric manufacturers, such as Moda, also identified one of the major quandaries facing the novice quilter: which fabrics can I put together to create the 'right effect'?

As a result, most patchwork fabrics now come as part of a range, or fabric grouping, where the colours, scale and design all complement one other.

The aim of this book is to start with the basics of patchwork and quilting: each lesson will take you through a technique you will come to use time and time again. The projects are all made using Moda's Charm Packs; each charm pack is a collection of pre-cut 5in squares of fabric from a particular range, so you can get straight on with the sewing, rather than having to deliberate over fabric choices. (Towards the end of the book you'll find a lesson on choosing fabrics, which will help you to take those first steps in making your own selections.) I hope that this book will take you on an exciting journey into a new creative hobby, and a world full of lovely quilting friends!

CONTENTS

 Introduction *page 3*
Basic Tools and Equipment *page 5*
Fabrics and Threads *page 6*

 **Lesson 1:** The Basics *page 9*
Project 1: Simple Charms *page 11*

 **Lesson 2:** Sashing and Borders *page 15*
Project 2: Sashed Charms *page 18*

 **Lesson 3:** Rotary Cutting *page 21*
Project 3: Charmed Magic *page 24*

 **Lesson 4:** Triangles and Other Tricks *page 27*
Project 4: Charming Triangles *page 31*

 **Lesson 5:** Wadding, Backing, Basting and Marking *page 34*
Project 5: Charmed Broken Squares *page 36*

 **Lesson 6:** Quilting *page 39*
Project 6: Star Charms *page 41*

 **Lesson 7:** Sewing Bias Seams, and Binding Quilts *page 45*
Project 7: Charmed Twist *page 47*

 **Lesson 8:** Simple Appliqué *page 51*
Project 8: Floating Flower Charms *page 55*

 **Lesson 9:** Choosing Fabrics *page 59*
Project 9: Basket of Charms *page 61*

 **Lesson 10:** Making Bow Tie Blocks *page 66*
Project 10: Bow Charming *page 67*

 Acknowledgements and Thanks *page 70*

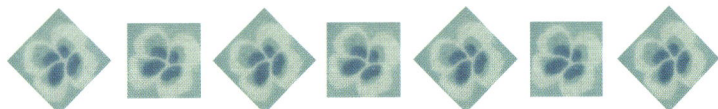

Basic Tools and Equipment

There are many gadgets and gizmos on sale in quilt shops, and if you're a beginner it can be difficult to know what you really ought to invest in and what is a non-essential luxury. In fact you can begin quilting with a very basic set of tools and equipment. I've put together below a list of absolute essentials – many of which you may well already have around the house or in your sewing box – and then a second list of items which are useful but not vital.

◆ Essential

- cotton thread
- iron and ironing board
- marking tools: pencils, chalk markers, wash-out pens
- needles: package of sharps (for hand piecing), assorted sizes; package of betweens (for hand quilting), size Nos 8-12
- pins
- rotary cutting tools:
  rotary cutter
  self-healing cutting mat with grid lines
  rotary ruler (a 6 x 24in ruler is best for cutting long strips)
- a selection of scissors:
  large, sharp scissors for fabric
  a pair for paper and card
  embroidery scissors (small, sharp-pointed ones) for trimming points, appliqué and cutting off loose threads
- seam ripper
- ruler with ¼in markings, or 'quilter's quarter'

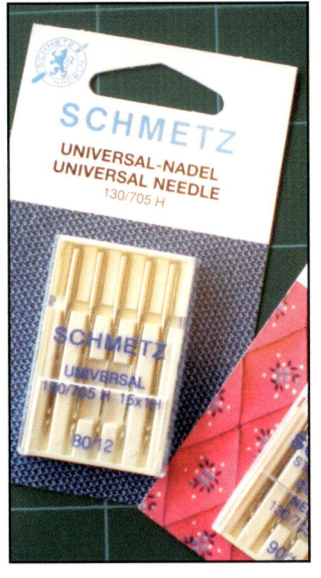

◆ Useful

- graph paper
- template plastic
- thimble to fit the middle finger of your sewing hand
- sewing machine, plus:
  assorted machine needles
  ¼in foot
  walking foot (sometimes called an even-feed foot)
- quilting hoop or frame for hand quilting

REMEMBER
Always put a fresh needle in your machine when you start to quilt; use a 70/10 or 70/11.

The traditional needles used for hand piecing and quilting are called betweens, and are generally smaller and stronger than normal sewing needles, so you can easily sew through a number of layers without the needle bending or breaking. A between has a very small eye, which prevents any extra bump at the eye of the needle when the thread is being pulled though the fabrics. Hand quilting needles are very strong and fine; they allow you to make very small stitches and to move the needle in any direction as you stitch.

Straight pins are needed for piecing. Flat-headed 'flower pins' are very fine, and are easier to use when you're piecing by machine.

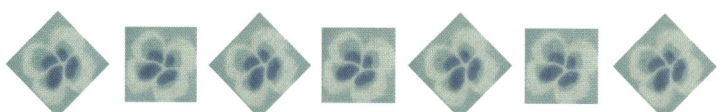

Fabrics and Threads

◆ Fabrics

Choosing the right fabrics for your quilt will determine how the quilt looks and how long it will last. Buy high-quality cotton fabric and you will enjoy working with it, your quilt will make up well, and it will look and feel wonderful. Try to avoid loose weaves and poor-quality fabric – you are going to spend many hours making your quilt, and you want it to last for years to come. Cheap cottons often fray badly, and are difficult to cut and piece accurately.

Most patchwork is done using cotton fabric, as it is available in thousands of prints and colours, it presses easily, and it handles well during sewing. The majority of fabrics on sale in specialised patchwork and quilting shops are 100% cotton, and approximately 44in wide on the bolt. Wider fabrics are available in a limited range, and these are normally used for quilt backings.

Alongside fabric for sale on the bolt, you will probably find that your local quilt shop has some pre-cut pieces of fabric. The most common pre-cut amount is a 'fat quarter,' where a half metre of fabric has been cut along the fold to make a piece approximately 22 x 18/19in. This rectangle is often more useful than a 'thin quarter,' which is simply a quarter-metre cut across the full width of the fabric bolt, producing a piece approximately 44 x 9in. Don't be afraid to ask for help when choosing your fabric in a quilt shop or at a show – most people working there are quilters and they know their stock!

Some manufacturers have also produced pre-cuts in other sizes. These packs enable you to use a wide range of several fabrics, all of which co-ordinate. The projects in this book are based around Moda Charm Packs, which are packs of pre-cut 5in squares. You can, of course, cut your own squares, but the charm packs take away the struggle of choosing fabrics as they generally follow these good principles of fabric selection:

- there is a good balance of pattern, colour and value
- the pack has a variety of prints – floral, paisley, dots, striped etc
- the prints have a good mix of size and scale
- tone-on-tone fabrics pick up one of the colours in the multicoloured fabrics

A selection of Moda Charm Packs

Some useful fabric terms

Selvedges are the densely-woven finished edges of the fabric. **Grain** refers to the direction of the woven threads. **Crosswise (weft) grain** runs at right angles to the selvedges and is slightly stretchy; **lengthwise (warp) grain** runs parallel to the selvedges and has virtually no stretch. **Bias grain** runs at 45° to the selvedges and has the greatest amount of stretch.

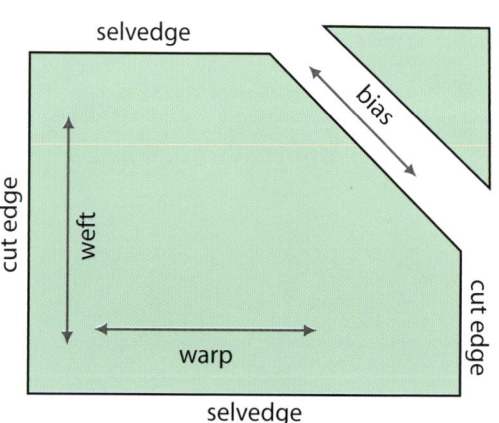

Should I pre-wash my fabrics?

Some quilters always pre-wash their fabrics, to ensure that no colour can bleed out when the quilt itself is washed, and to make sure that there is no shrinkage. I rarely pre-wash my fabrics, unless I am worried about the colour-fastness of particular ones, such as red batiks. If you do pre-wash your fabrics they will lose some of their sizing – the slight starchiness that makes them easier to mark and cut. If you are pre-washing, use spray starch to reintroduce a bit of 'body' while the fabric is slightly damp.

Moda pre-cut fabrics are not meant to be pre-washed – it can result in fraying, and you'll find it much easier to produce the quilts in this book if you don't pre-wash.

This is probably the best place to mention the cross-over between metric and imperial measurements in the quilting world. Because we buy fabrics in metric (metres, centimetres etc) in the UK, this is how I'll be specifying the amounts you need for each project. However, virtually all quilting designs – and most of the quilting rulers, cutting mats etc – are based on the imperial measurements (inches), and when accurate piecing is required, it's impossible give exact conversions. Therefore, I'll be using imperial measurements within the patterns themselves.

◆ Threads

Always try to use cotton thread when sewing cotton fabric. Polyester thread is much tougher and it pulls against the cotton fibres in the fabric; over time, the cotton will wear and tear. For machine piecing, use a neutral thread such as light/medium grey.

A selection of general sewing threads

There are many different weights and types of cotton thread available, but, as a simple rule, use a medium-weight (40) cotton for hand or machine piecing.

Quilting thread is sold as either 'hand quilting thread,' or 'machine quilting/machine embroidery thread'. You can use a machine thread to quilt by hand, but not vice-versa.

Various hand quilting threads

Assorted machine quilting threads

REMEMBER
Don't use hand quilting thread in your sewing machine; choose a specific machine quilting or machine embroidery thread.

The Basics

In this lesson we'll look at the basic techniques which will be used for virtually every quilt you make: cutting, seam allowances, piecing and pressing. We're going to begin by having a look at making templates, which is a useful skill to learn for future quilt projects; most of the quilts in this book do not need templates, but many other patterns do.

◆ Templates

To make a template, trace the shape onto graph paper or template plastic. Use a ruler to draw any straight lines, and make sure the corners are square. If you are using graph paper, draw the shape onto the paper, cut it out roughly then glue it onto card. Once the glue has dried, cut out the shape on the marked lines. Be very accurate at this stage! Measure your template before you use it to make sure that it is the correct size. Label all your templates with grain arrows and size.

To use the template, place it on the wrong side of the fabric and draw around it with a sharp pencil – these are the sewing lines (**a**). Remove the template and measure the marked shape to make sure that the template hasn't slipped. When you are drawing squares and triangles, mark a point at each corner of the shape with an obvious dot – this will be useful when you are matching shapes to pin them together. Before you can cut out the shape you also need to measure and mark the seam allowances. Using a quilt rule with a ¼in marking, draw lines ¼in outside the boundaries of the shape (**b**), and cut out the fabric on these lines (**c**).

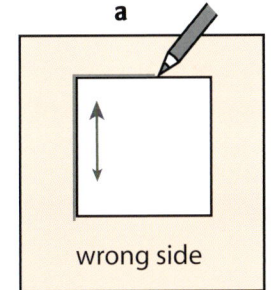

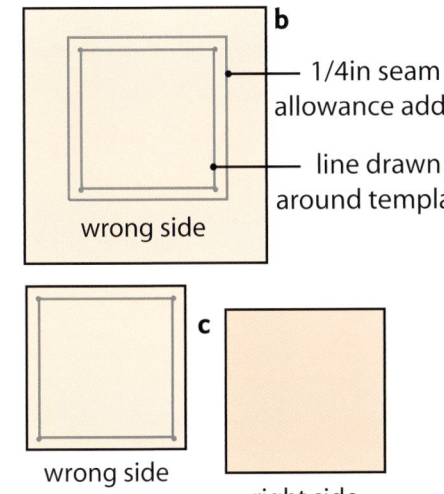

◆ Cutting

Measure twice: cut once! Once you have marked the patchwork shapes and their seam allowances on the back of the fabric, cut the shapes out along outside lines using sharp fabric scissors.

>>>

REMEMBER
Measure twice: cut once!

>>>

◆ Seam allowances

The normal seam allowance for quilt making is ¼in (6mm): all the piecing measurements for projects in this book include this ¼in seam allowance. If you stitch an accurate ¼in seam, you will have success and satisfaction in quilting. If you don't, you will experience frustration and will often have to resort to using your seam ripper …

◆ Hand piecing

When you are piecing by hand, place the two pieces of fabric to be joined right sides together; pin through and match any marked dots (see the section on templates above), and along the stitching lines, placing pins at right angles to the sewing line (**a**).

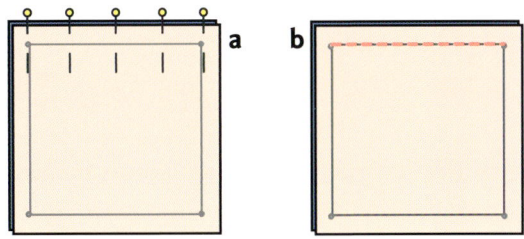

Use a single strand of cotton thread. Backstitch to secure the thread into the fabric (avoid knots, as these create bumps and can become unravelled), and sew with small, even running stitches along the marked sewing lines (**b**). Finish your seam with another backstitch and trim the thread – don't sew into the seam allowance. If you have to sew over seams, then make a backstitch either side of the overlap to reinforce the seam.

◆ Machine piecing

Your machine should be in good working order, with a straight stitch and even tension. Machine piecing is fast and gives a very strong seam, but the success of your quilt depends on sewing accurate and consistent ¼in seams. Either purchase a ¼in foot for your machine, or mark a seam guide by using ¼in masking tape – stick a piece on the throat plate of your machine, ¼in to the right of the needle.

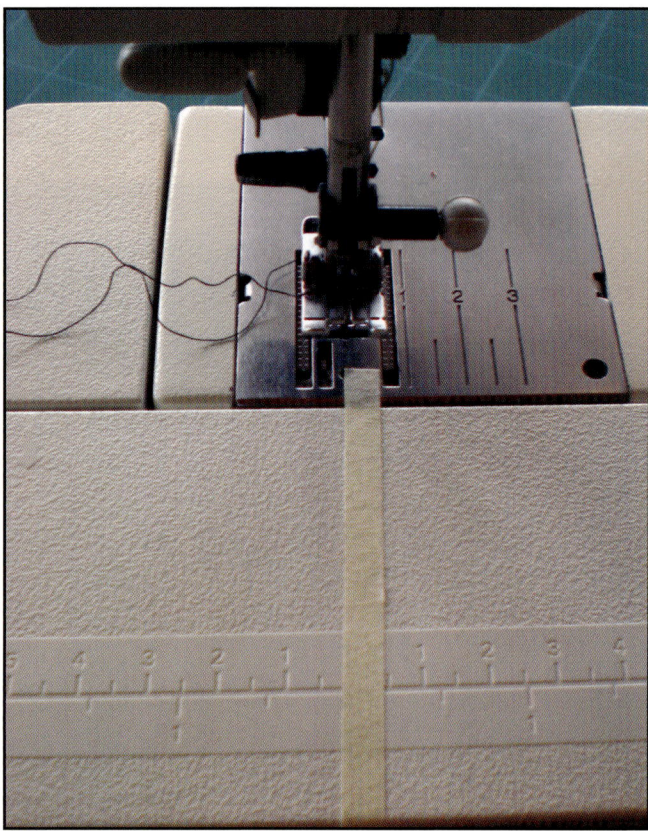

Masking tape marking a ¼in seam line

REMEMBER
Check the accuracy of your seam guide on sample strips before sewing your quilt.

To machine piece, use straight stitch and set the stitch length to 2-2.5. Place the two pieces of fabric to be joined right sides together, aligning the raw edges. Before you start to join these pieces, feed a small scrap of fabric under the needle and sew part-way through it, stopping just before the end of the scrap (**a**).

Place the fabric pair in front of the presser foot and continue stitching (without lifting the presser foot or cutting the thread). This method of starting on a scrap of fabric will prevent threads and fabric from being caught in the foot plate.

As you sew the fabric pieces together, gently guide the fabric with your hands and check that it feeds through the machine evenly and without slipping. If you want to pin pieces together before you sew, then make sure the pins are at right angles to the sewing line, and remove the pins just before you reach them.

Chain-piecing is a quick way to sews several units in succession. Feed the pieces under the presser foot, one after another (**b**), with a few stitches in between (without cutting the threads or lifting the foot), and then cut them apart when the chain is complete. Finish the chain by sewing onto a piece of scrap fabric, ready to start the next chain.

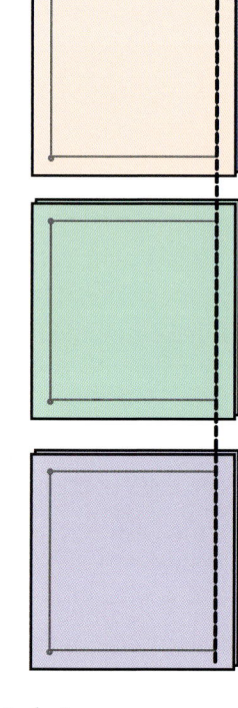

◆ Pressing

It is important to press your work as it progresses, especially if you are piecing by machine, because it will then move under the presser foot easily. Press your work by placing the iron up and down on the fabric rather than sliding it over the pieces. Start pressing with a dry iron – use steam with caution as this can distort the fabric.

As a general rule, press the seams towards the dark fabric, but at intersections (eg when joining rows together), press seams in opposite directions as shown below; this allows opposing seams to butt up together, which will help to produce a flat join and reduce bulk.

Simple Charms

This delightful quilt couldn't be easier to stitch – so even if you're a complete beginner, you'll find that you've put together the quilt top in a jiffy.

Finished size: 39½in (100cm) square
Charm pack featured: Santorini

You will need

- ◇ One charm pack (containing at least thirty-six 5in squares)
- ◇ 25cm (thin quarter-metre) of toning fabric for the inner border
- ◇ 50cm contrast fabric for the outer border
- ◇ 30cm fabric for the binding
- ◇ 1.1m backing fabric
- ◇ wadding: crib size (or at least 45in/115cm square)

Instructions

Use ¼in seams throughout

To assemble the central design

1 Sort the charm pack squares into a 6 x 6 layout, making sure that you have a good mixture of colours and patterns across the design (**a**).

a

2 Stitch the bottom row of 6 squares together, making sure that you keep them in the right order (**b**). Repeat with the remaining five rows (**c**).

b
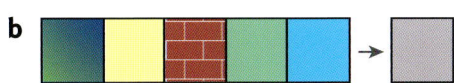

c
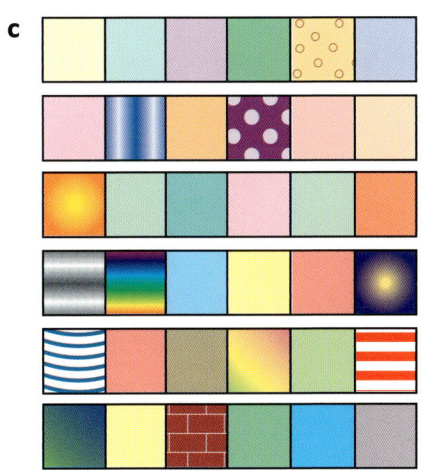

d

e

3 Press all the seams in the first row in one direction, and all the seams in the second row in the opposite direction. Pin the rows together so that the seams meet, and stitch (**d**). Add the other rows to the design in the same way (**e**).

To create the quilt top

4 Once you have sewn all 36 squares together, measure the quilt top; it should measure 27½in. (It doesn't matter if it's smaller – simply adjust the lengths of your border strips accordingly.) Cut the inner border fabric into four 2½in strips. Cut two of these strips to 27½in long, and the other two to 31½in long. Sew one of the shorter strips to the top of the quilt and one to the bottom (**f**). Stitch the remaining strips to the sides of the design (**g**).

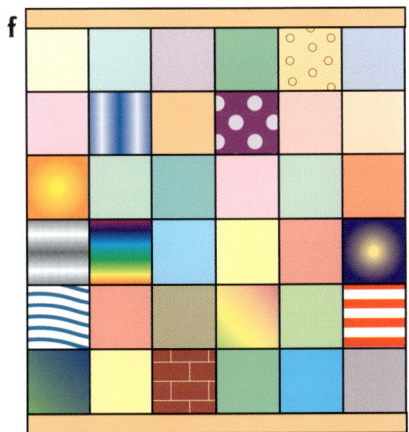

5 Measure the quilt again: it should now be 31½in square. Cut the outer border fabric into four 4½in strips. Cut two of these to measure 31½in long and add them to the top and bottom of the quilt. Cut the remaining two strips to 39½in and add them to the sides of the quilt (**h**). Your quilt top is now complete.

Quilting

6 Follow the instructions on page 35 for layering your quilt top with the wadding and backing.

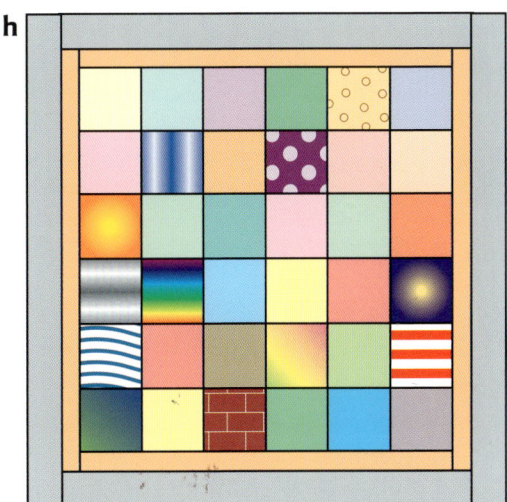

7 Quilt the layers simply, working from the centre outwards. There are various methods that are quick and effective:

- use several strands of embroidery cotton and tie a decorative knot at the corner of each square patch
- stitch a button through the layers at the corner of each square patch
- quilt by hand or machine 'in the ditch' – just alongside the seams
- quilt diagonal lines by hand or machine across the squared quilt centre

8 Follow the instructions on page 46 for binding the edges of the quilt.

Make it bigger!

You can easily make this basic quilt design larger by alternating the patterned charm squares with plain squares in a co-ordinating fabric. This will give you a 50in (127cm) square quilt.

You will need

- ◇ One charm pack (containing at least 42 5in squares)
- ◇ 70cm co-ordinating plain fabric
- ◇ 70cm border fabric
- ◇ 2.75m backing fabric
- ◇ 1.4m wadding, or a piece at least 54in square

From the plain fabric cut 40 5in squares. Make up nine rows of nine squares (a total of 81 squares), alternating the plain and patterned squares as shown in the photograph below. The size of the quilt top at this stage will be 41in square.

From the border fabric, cut five strips measuring 5in x the width of the fabric. Cut two of these to 41in long and sew them to the top and bottom of the quilt. Cut one of the remaining strips in half, and join one half to each of the other full-length strips. Cut these border strips down to 50in, and sew them to the sides of the quilt. Layer, quilt and bind as before.

The Simple Charms design made larger by alternating the charm squares with plain squares in a chequerboard design.

LESSON 2

Sashing and Borders

◆ Sashing

Sashing describes the plain or patterned fabric strips that are commonly sewn between quilt blocks. Sashing helps to frame the blocks, so they have definition and stand out on their own. The sashing can be simple strips, or it can be pieced and used as part of the quilt design.

The width of the sashing strips depends on the size of the blocks – if you use wide sashing strips with small blocks then the sashing will be out of proportion for the quilt. So, for 5in charm squares, I suggest you cut sashing strips 1½ or 2in wide. On a quilt with larger blocks, for example 12in blocks, the sashing would normally be cut 2½in wide.

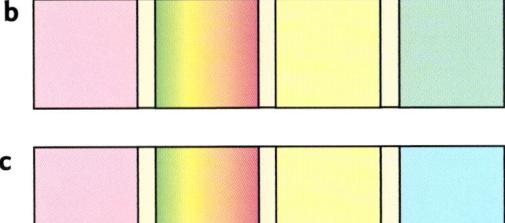
b

c

d

Adding sashing

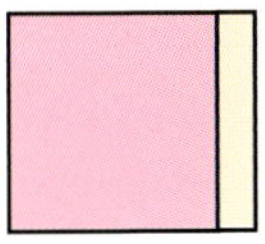

1. Before you can start to attach the sashing, it is important to make sure that all the blocks are a consistent size. (You'll find full instructions for squaring up blocks in Lesson 4, see page 29.) Once you have decided on the width of sashing, including the seam allowances, cut a sashing strip to that width and the same length as the block. Stitch the sashing strip to the block down one side using a ¼in seam (**a**). Press the seams towards the block.

a

2. Continue sewing on sashing strips and blocks until all the blocks in a row have been joined together (**b**). Repeat the process on the other rows in the quilt.

Measure the length of the finished row, and cut long sashing strips to this length (joining strips of fabric if necessary to achieve the required length). Sew these long sashing strips to the rows to join the rows together (**c**), taking care to pin carefully so that the blocks line up correctly, then press the seams towards the blocks, away from the sashing.

3. Corner stones, or setting squares, are squares of fabric that are pieced within the sashing strips and fit into the corners of the blocks (**d**). They add more interest to the quilt, and help in lining up the blocks and keeping the quilt square.

◆ Borders

Borders are important! They frame and contain the design used in the quilt top, and they are a definite boundary that leads the eye back to the centre of the quilt.

Measurements for cutting borders accompany all the patterns in this book, but if you want to adapt the size of the quilt make sure that you measure the quilt as described below.

Adding an overlapped border

1 Measure the length of the quilt top through the centre (**a**), and cut the side borders to this length. Use a pin to mark the centre of each side border strip and the centre of each side of the quilt top (**b**).

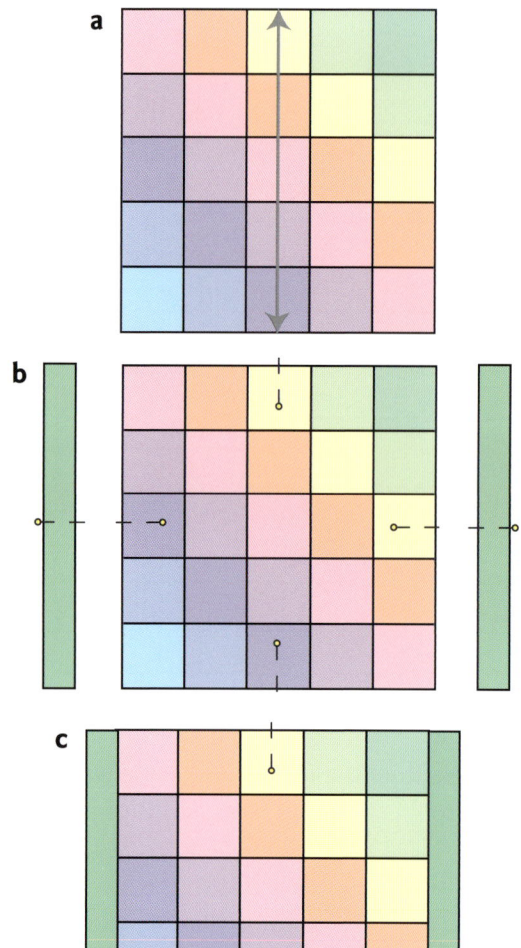

3 Measure the width of the quilt including the side borders, and cut the top and bottom borders to this measurement. Pin and sew the top and bottom borders as described in steps 1 and 2, and press the seams towards the borders (**d**).

Adding a mitred border

1 Measure the width of the quilt, then cut the top and bottom border strips to this measurement + twice the border width + 3in for seams and ease of handling (**a**). Mark with a pin the centre of the border strip, and the centre of the quilt top.

2 With right sides together, pin the borders to the quilt top, matching the centre points and outer edges. Stitch using a ¼in seam; press the seam allowances towards the borders (**c**).

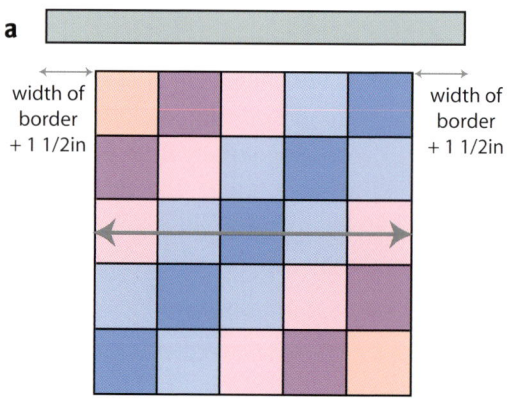

width of border + 1 1/2in

width of border + 1 1/2in

On the border strip, working outwards from the centre pin in each direction, measure and mark one half of the width of the quilt top (**b**).

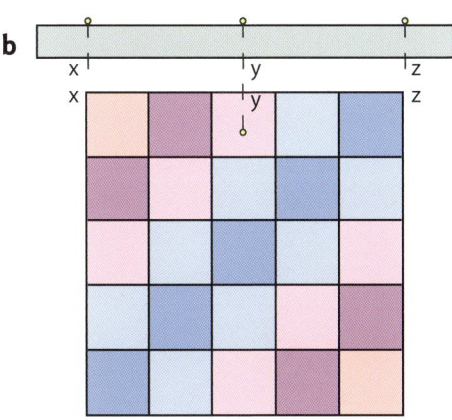

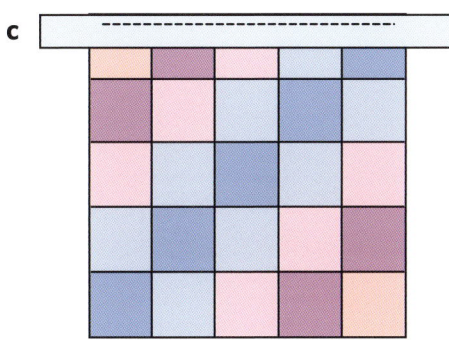

2 Place the top border strip and the quilt top right sides together, matching the centre points, and matching the outer pins to the raw edges of the quilt top. Sew the border strip to the quilt top using a ¼in seam; start and end ¼in from the corners of the quilt top (**c**). Press the seam towards the border, and repeat for the bottom border (**d**).

3 Cut the side border strips to measure the length of the quilt + twice the border width + 3in for seams and ease of handling. Use the same method to add the side borders (**e**).

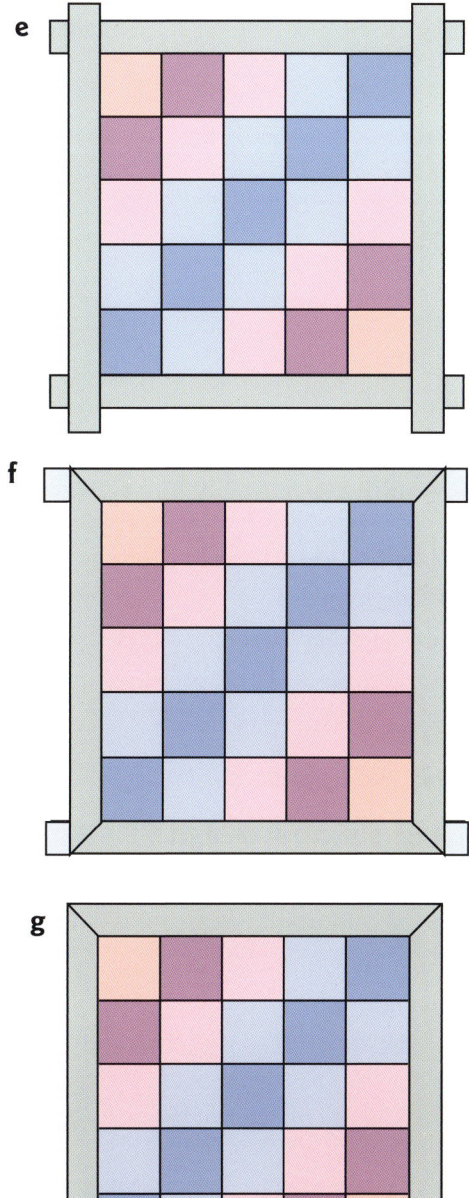

4 To make the mitres, lay the quilt top on a flat surface, right side up, and lay one border strip over the other at each corner. Fold under the top strip at a 45° angle; press the fold, pin and then slipstitch in place (**f**). On the wrong side, trim the corner seams to ¼in (**g**).

Sashed Charms

This quilt moves your skills on to using sashing in a simple design; once you have mastered the technique, you will be able to sash larger quilts too.

Finished size: 43in (109cm) square
Charm pack featured: Rouenneries

You will need

◇ One charm pack (containing at least 36 5in squares)
◇ 50cm contrast fabric for the sashing
◇ 50cm border fabric
◇ 40cm fabric for the binding
◇ 1.2m backing fabric, at least 44in wide (this measurement is quite tight; if your quilt comes out a little larger, you'll need to buy 2.4m backing fabric and join two pieces as described on page 34, which will leave some fabric left over once you've cut the backing pieces).
◇ 1.2m square wadding

Instructions

Use ¼in seams throughout

To assemble the central design

1 Lay out the squares in a 6 x 6 pattern, so that there's a good mix of colour and design across the layout.

2 From the sashing fabric, cut four strips 2in wide x the width of the fabric. Trim off the selvedges from the ends of the strips and then cut each one into 5in segments (**a**). (You should be able to cut eight of these 5 x 2in segments from each strip).

3 Starting with the top row of squares, sew one of these sashing strips to the right-hand side of every square, except the last one in the row at the right-hand end. Following the instructions for adding sashing (see page 15), sew the square/sashing pairs together to form each row (**b**). Repeat this with the other five rows.

4 Measure the length of a row: it should be 35in. From the sashing fabric, cut five more strips measuring 2in x the width of the fabric. Remove the selvedges, and cut these sashing strips down to the length of the rows (ie 35in).

5 Carefully pin one of these long strips to the bottom of the first row of squares; stitch in place (**c**).

Take the second row of squares and pin the top of this row to the other side of the sashing strip you have just attached, taking care to line up the squares in adjoining rows: stitch. Repeat this method until all six rows have been joined with sashing in between (**d**). Measure the size of the quilt top – it should now be 35in square.

PROJECT 2

To create the quilt top

6 Cut the border fabric into four strips measuring 4½in x the width of the fabric. Cut down the top and bottom border strip to 35in and sew to the top and bottom of the quilt. Cut the side strips to 43in and sew to the sides of the quilt (**e**).

Your quilt top is now complete; layer it with the wadding and backing fabric, then quilt and bind as you wish.

e

Make it bigger!

You can make the Sashed Charms quilt a little bigger (46in/117cm square) by also adding sashing strips to the top, bottom and sides of the quilt top before you add the borders.

You will need

◇ One charm pack containing at least 36 5in squares
◇ 70cm contrasting fabric for the sashing
◇ 70cm border fabric
◇ 40cm binding fabric
◇ 2.6m backing fabric
◇ 1.3m square wadding

1 To make the bigger version, you will need another four sashing strips each measuring 2in x the width of the fabric. Make up the quilt top as described above, but before you add the borders, cut two of these extra sashing strips to 35in long and add them to the top and bottom of the quilt. Cut the remaining two sashing strips to 38in and sew to the sides of the quilt (**a**).

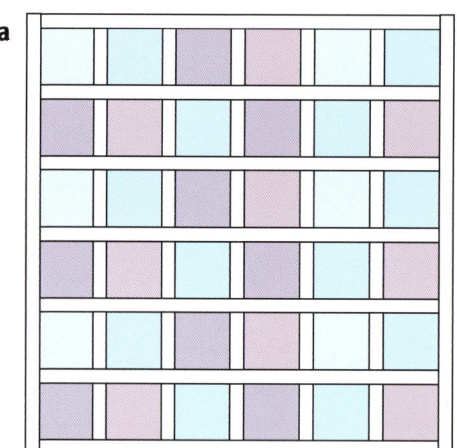

a

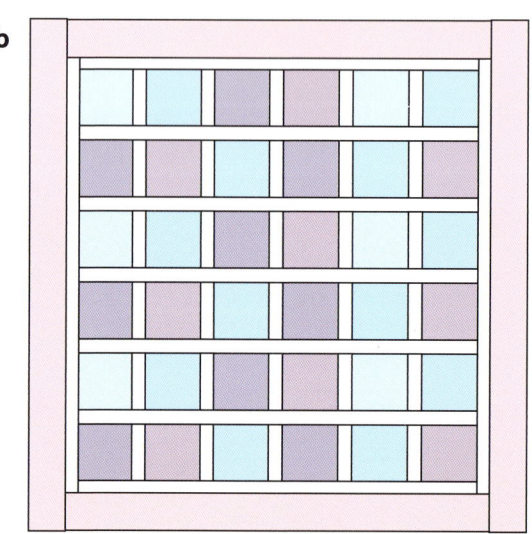

b

2 Cut the border fabric into five strips measuring 4½in x the width of the fabric. Cut two of the strips down to 38in and sew these to the top and bottom of the quilt. Cut one of the remaining strips in half, and join one half to each of the other two border strips. Cut these new strips down to 46in and sew them to the sides of the quilt top (**b**).

On this quilt you can see the extra sashing around the edges

Rotary Cutting

Rotary cutting is one of the most time-saving skills you can learn, because it removes the need to mark and cut individual pieces of fabric. So, it speeds up piecing the quilt, and – if you use the method correctly – it will improve the accuracy of your piecing. Another great bonus is that you can cut several layers of fabric at a time; don't try and cut too many layers together, though, as the finished pieces will not be so accurate.

Rotary cutters look like pizza cutters, but the blades are razor-sharp! There are several types of rotary cutter available, featuring different-sized blades, various handle shapes, and the option of a protective guard for the blade. If you're new to rotary cutting, I would suggest beginning with a medium-sized rotary cutter with a 45mm replaceable blade.

◆ Preparing the fabric

Assuming that you are working with the full width of your fabric (normally 44in), fold the fabric in half lengthwise and match the selvedges. With the bulk of the fabric on your left (assuming you are right-handed), place a long quilters' ruler across the fabric, matching one of the horizontal line markings to the fold. Cut off about ½in from the raw edge of the fabric to give a straight edge to measure from (**a**).

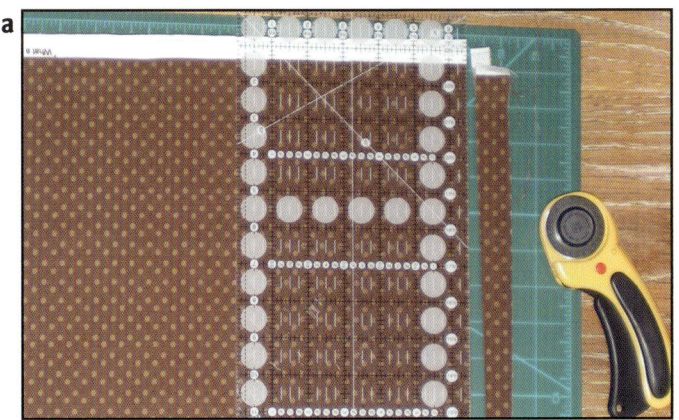

◆ Cutting strips

Turn the fabric (or board) around, so that the bulk of fabric is now on your right and the trimmed edge on the left. Always measure and cut from a trimmed edge, using the measurement marking on the ruler. To cut strips, align the appropriate measurement on your ruler with the left (trimmed) edge of the fabric. For example, to cut a 2½in strip, place the 2½in line of the edge of the fabric (**b**).

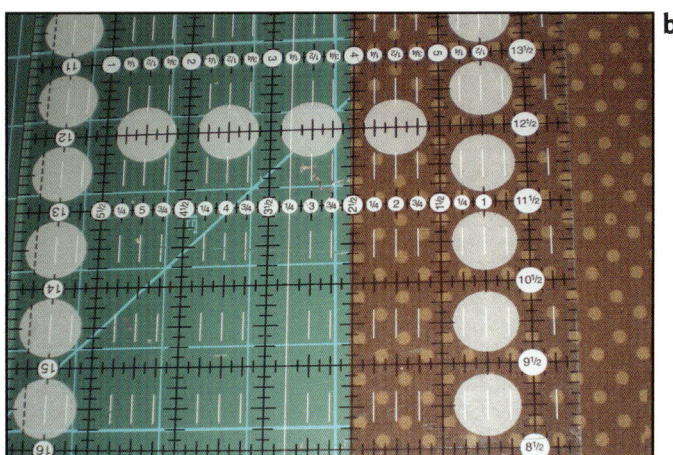

Place your left hand firmly on the ruler, and start to cut the fabric, starting at the bottom (nearest to you). For safety, always cut away from your body. As you cut up the fabric 'walk' your left-hand fingers up the ruler, maintaining pressure on it so that the fabric does not slip (**c**). While you are using the rotary cutter, ensure that you keep the fingers of your other hand well away from the blade.

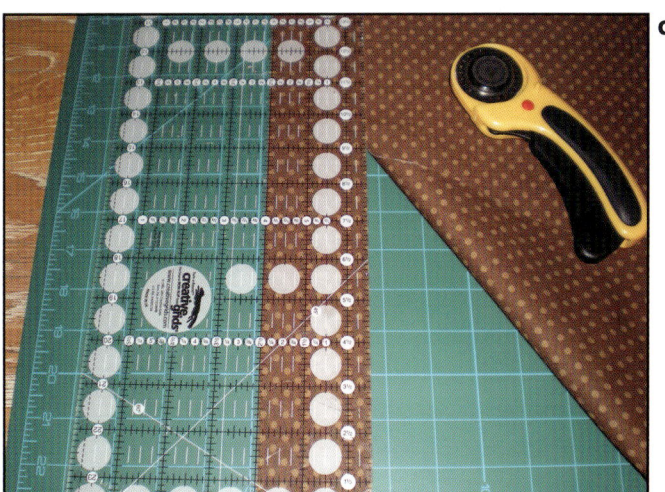

REMEMBER
Always use a rotary cutter with the correct mat, and don't use an ordinary classroom or metal ruler: the cutters are very sharp, and can slip if not used with the right equipment.

◆ Cutting squares and rectangles

To cut individual squares, cut a strip to the required width and trim off the selvedge edges. Turn the strip around by 90° and, using the appropriate measurement on your ruler, measure from the left edge of the fabric and cut the squares (**d**). Use a similar method to cut rectangles; cut a strip to the size of the width of the rectangles first, and then sub-cut it into the length of the rectangles (**e**).

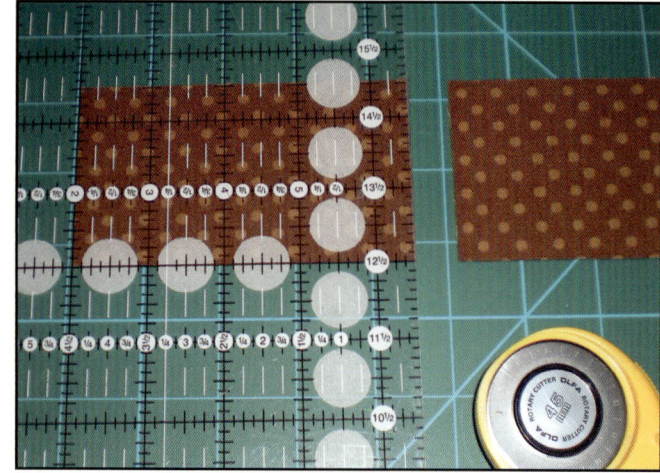

◆ Cutting larger pieces

Square off the edge of the fabric. You will then need to use two rulers – one long and the other square – for extra-wide strips. Suppose you wanted to cut a strip measuring 15in, then first determine the width of the longest ruler (normally 6½in) and take that away from the width you want to cut – in this example this will leave 8½in. Find the 8½in marking on the second (square) ruler, and line this up along the straight edge (**f**). Place the long ruler next to it on the right-hand side, and this will give you the total length of 15in from the left-hand edge.

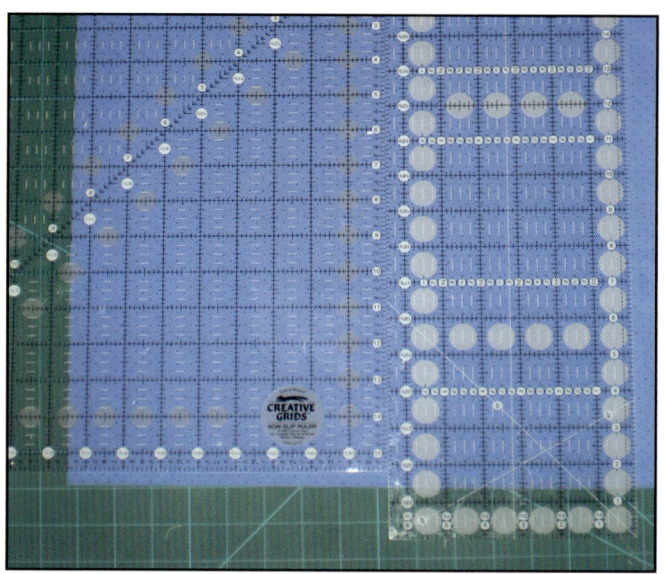

Slide the square ruler up and down the straight edge to ensure that the long ruler is correctly positioned, and then cut along the right-hand edge of the long ruler.

In a similar way, you can sub-cut the wide strip into squares, rectangles and triangles.

◆ Cutting triangles

The easiest way to rotary-cut several right-angled triangles is to cut a square and then sub-cut the square into half-square or quarter-square triangles. This method is fully described in Lesson 4 – see page 27.

◆ Cutting diamonds or parallelograms

Make a paper template and use masking tape to fix it temporarily to the back of your rotary-cutting ruler, aligning one edge of the template along one edge of the ruler (**g**).

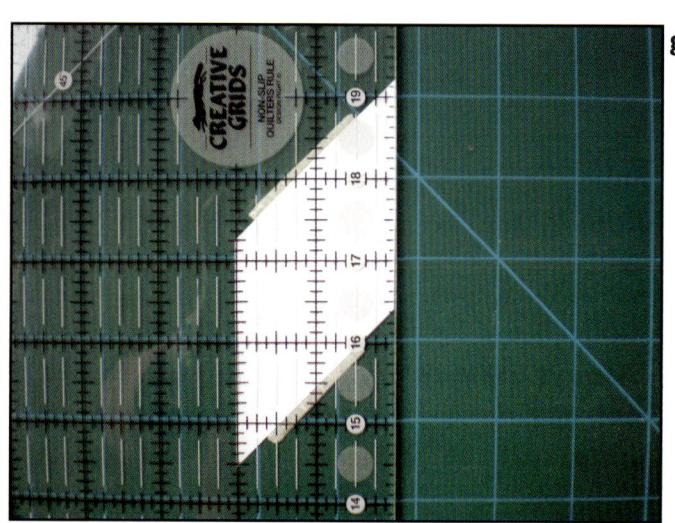

Cut a fabric strip the same width as the template, and then lay the ruler on the fabric strip with the template and fabric edges aligned. Trim off the end of the strip (**h**).

Turn the ruler round so that the template is now at the bottom of the ruler, and align it with the cut edge. Move along the fabric strip, cutting diamonds (**i** and **j**) or parallelograms.

◆ Cutting trapezoids

In a similar way to above, make a paper template and fix it to the back face of your ruler, aligning one edge (with both angles) along the edge of the ruler.

Cut a fabric strip the same width as the template. Place the ruler on the fabric strip with the template and fabric edges aligned (**k**); cut off the end of the strip (**l**) and cut at the other side to make the first trapezoid (**m**).

Turn the ruler round to cut the next trapezoid, and continue in this way all along the fabric strip.

Charmed Magic

Traditional nine-patch blocks are the stars of this quilt. A standard nine-patch block is created from nine equal-sized squares of fabric, arranged in three rows of three – charm squares are ideal!

Finished size: 52½in (135cm) square
Charm pack featured: Essence

You will need

◇ Two charm packs (containing at least 72 5in squares)
◇ Fat quarter of contrast fabric
◇ 25cm fabric for the inner border (ideally the same fabric that you've used as the contrast)
◇ 60cm fabric for the outer border
◇ 40cm fabric for the binding
◇ 2.9m backing fabric
◇ Wadding, at least 1.4m square

Instructions

Use ¼in seams throughout

To assemble the central design

1 Cut nine 5in squares from the contrast fabric. Sort the charm squares into nine groups of 8 fabrics, with a good mix of colour and print size. Take one of these groups, and lay the fabrics out in a 3 x 3 pattern, with one of the contrast squares in the middle (**a**). For maximum contrast, try to get four darker prints and four lighter prints arranged with the darker prints in the corners of the nine-patch. Repeat this process for the other eight groups of patches.

2 Stitch the patches together in each block, first of all in rows of three (**b**), then joining the rows. Make sure that you keep the rows in the right order as you join them, so that the contrast fabric is in the centre (**c**).

3 Using a rotary cutter and ruler, measure vertically 2¼in from the inner seam of one block and cut it in half (**d**). Now make a similar cut across the block horizontally (**e**). You will now have four small blocks, each measuring 7in square. Repeat this with the other eight nine-patch blocks, to generate a total of 36 smaller blocks.

4 Arrange the blocks in six rows of six. There are various ways in which you can arrange these blocks to create different designs; I've used the layout shown in the diagrams (**f** and **g**), which requires turning some of the blocks by 180°.

5 Starting with the first row, stitch the blocks together (**h**); the finished row should measure 39½in. Repeat with the other five rows, then stitch the rows together (**i**, overleaf).

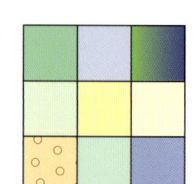
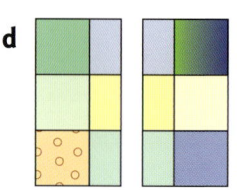
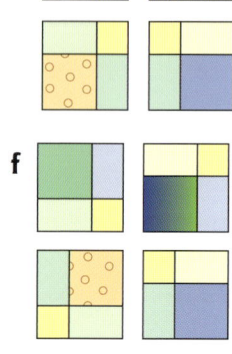

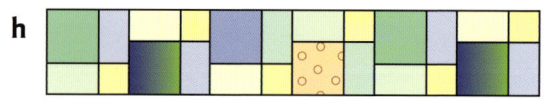

PROJECT 3

PROJECT 3

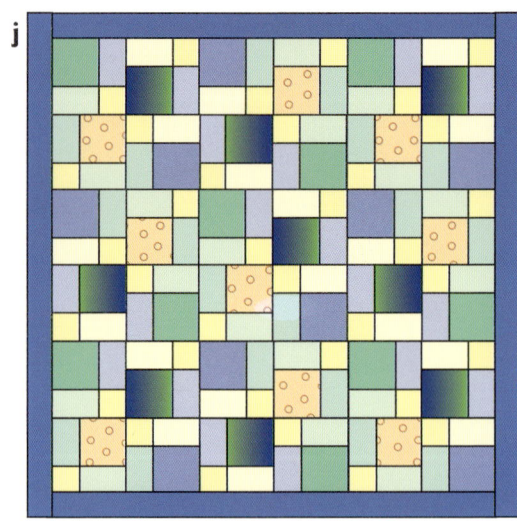

The Charmed Magic design in a different colourway

To create the quilt top

6 For the inner border, cut four strips measuring 2½in x the width of the fabric. Trim two of these strips to 39½in and stitch to the top and bottom of the quilt. Trim the other two to 43½in and sew to the sides of the quilt (**j**).

7 For the outer border, cut five strips each measuring 5in x the width of the fabric. Trim two of these strips down to 43½in and stitch to the top and bottom of the quilt. Cut one of remaining strips in half and sew one half to each of the other strips. Cut these new strips down to 52½in and stitch to the sides of the quilt (**k**).

Your quilt top is now complete; layer it with the wadding and backing fabric, then quilt and bind as you wish.

26

Triangles and Other Tricks

In this lesson we look at several more time-saving tips which will be useful for many of your quilts. First of all we'll explore accurate ways of cutting half-square and quarter-square triangles – patches which are used in many block designs. Then we'll cover quick methods of creating half-square and quarter-square triangle units. Finally we'll look at how to square up blocks.

◆ Half-square triangles

A half-square triangle is a right-angled triangle that has the bias grain of the fabric on the long side (**a**). You make a half-square triangle by cutting a square along one of the diagonals (**b**).

OK so far, you may say – but how do I work out the size of square that will give me a particular-sized triangle? Easy: the calculations for your square are based on the finished size of your half-square triangle unit (**c**). So, your first step is to work out your finished unit size. Then you add ⅞in. That's it: you simply add ⅞in to the required finished size of your half-square triangle unit.

So, for example, if you want a half-square triangle with finished short edges of 4in (so that you can join two of them to make a 4in square), you need to start with a 4⅞in square and cut it diagonally (**d**). If you stitch two of these half-square triangles together along the longest (bias) edge, you will make a square measuring 4½in (**e**) (ie finished size 4in).

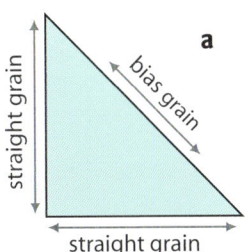
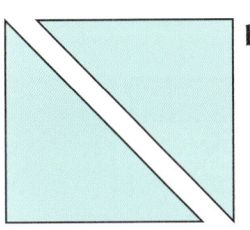
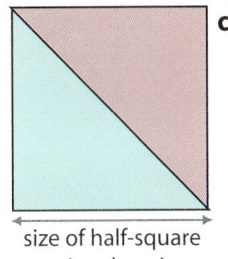
size of half-square triangle unit
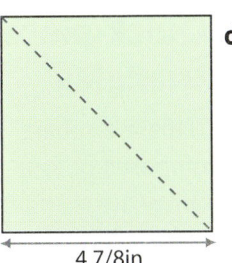
4 7/8in
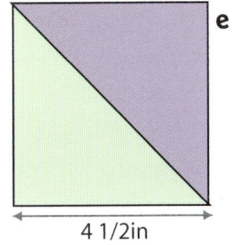
4 1/2in

◆ Quarter-square triangles

A quarter-square triangle is a right-angled triangle that has the bias of the fabric on the two short sides (**a**). You make a quarter-square triangle by cutting a square along both diagonals (**b**). Once again, the calculations for the size of your original square are based on the finished size of the unit (**c**). So, your first step is to work out your finished unit size, then you add 1¼in.

So, for example, if you want a quarter-square triangle with finished long edges of 4in (so that you can join four of them to make a 4in square), you need to start with a 5¼in square and cut it diagonally in both directions. If you stitch two of these quarter-square triangles together along the short sides (the bias edges) you will make a half-square triangle measuring 4⅞ on the short sides (**d**). If you sew four of the quarter-square triangles together you will make a square measuring 4½in (**e**) (ie finished size 4in).

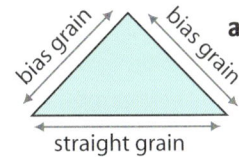
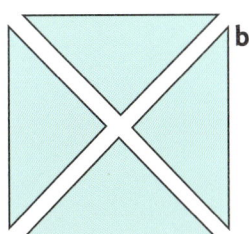
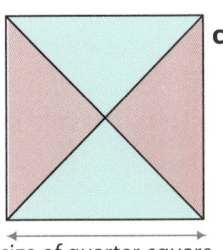
size of quarter-square triangle unit
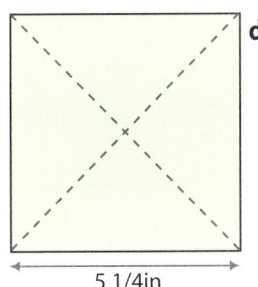
5 1/4in

4 1/2in

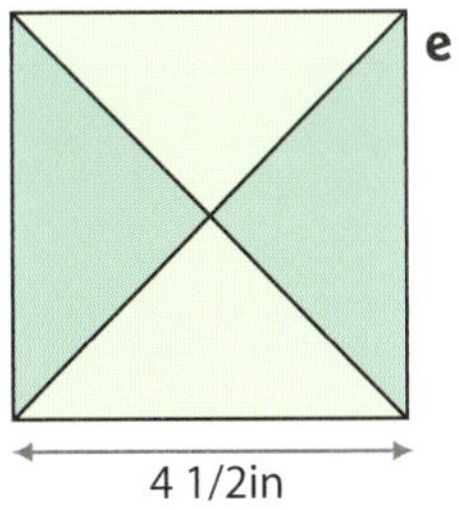

◆ Quick-pieced half-square triangles

Here's an easy method to make two identical squares, each containing two half-square triangles, which means that you don't have to stitch a seam between bias edges.

1 From each fabric, cut a square ⅞in larger than the finished size of the stitched unit. Draw a diagonal line on the back of the lighter-coloured square, then draw stitching lines ¼in each side of the diagonal (**a**).

27

LESSON 4

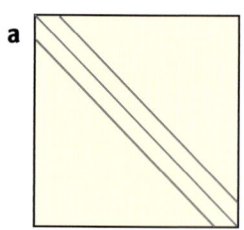 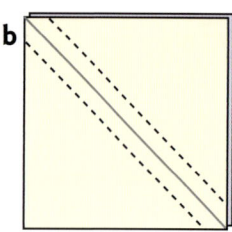

Place this on top of the other patterned square, right sides together, and sew along the two stitching lines (**b**) (not the centre diagonal).

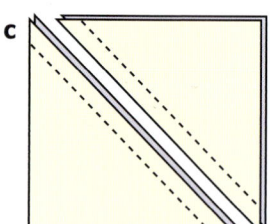 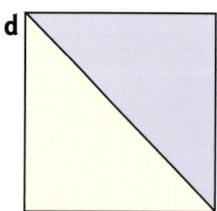

2 Use a rotary cutter to cut along the diagonal line (**c**), and open out each square (**d**). Press the seam allowances towards the darker fabric on each unit.

HINT
If you find that your finished unit is not accurate, cut your initial squares a little larger and trim the blocks to size once you have made them.

◆ Multiple half-square triangles

1 To make several units at a time, draw a grid of squares on the back of the lighter-coloured fabric, where the squares are 1in bigger than the finished units (**a**).

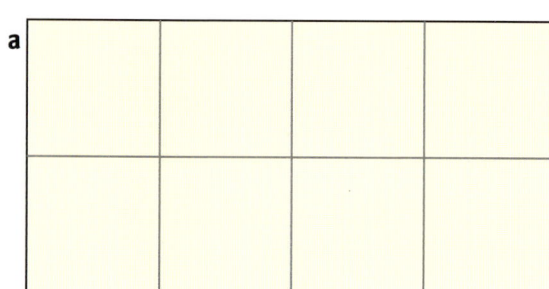

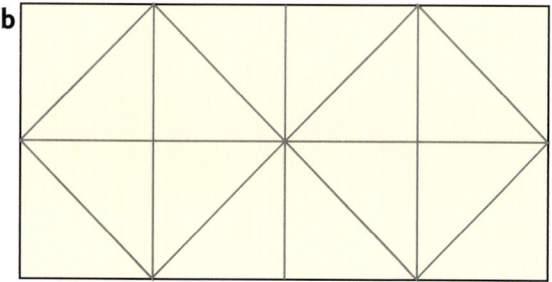

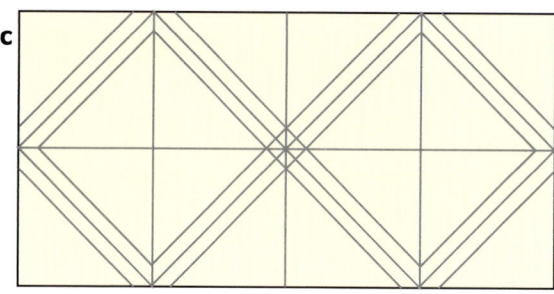

2 Draw diagonal lines on the grid as shown (**b**), then stitching lines ¼in either side of the diagonal lines (**c**).

3 Sew along all the stitching lines (**d**). Cut along all the diagonal lines, and the horizontal and vertical lines of the grid (**e**).

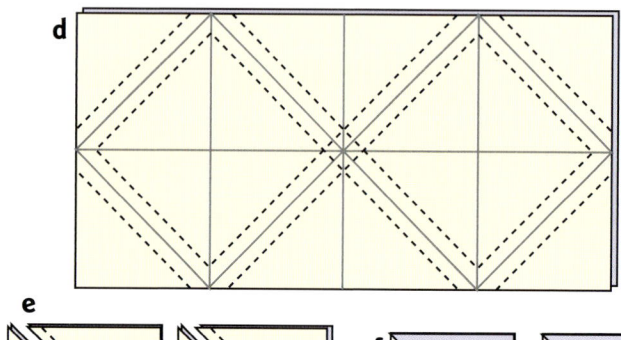

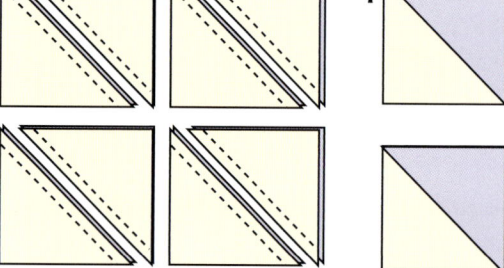 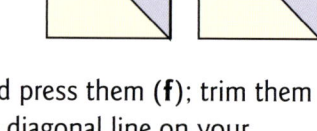

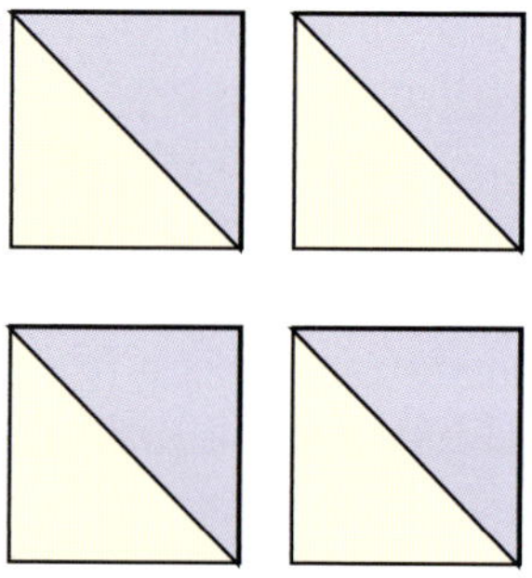

4 Open out the blocks and press them (**f**); trim them to size, making sure the diagonal line on your square ruler is lined up with the diagonal seam.

◆ Quick-pieced quarter-square triangles

1 To make a square composed of four quarter-square triangles, firstly make two of the half-square triangle units as described above (**a**). Put the two pieces right sides together, alternating the colours (**b**), with the diagonal seams aligned and pressed in opposite directions.

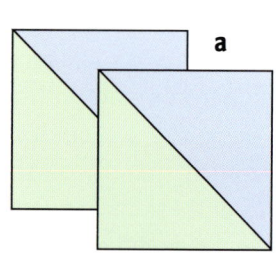

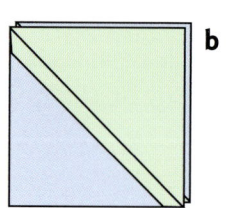

28

2 On the back of one of these units, draw another diagonal line, at right angles to the seam; draw a stitching line ¼in to each side of the diagonal (**c**).

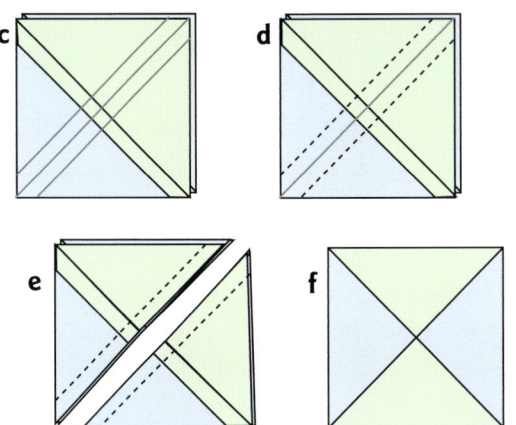

3 Sew along the stitching lines either side of the marked diagonal (**d**), then again cut them apart on the marked line (**e**). Open up the two triangles (**f**) and press the seams towards the darker fabric.

◆ Squaring up a block

Once you've pieced a block, it's important to square it up before you join it to other blocks or sashing; this process removes any slight inaccuracies or distortions that have crept in during the piecing. Your rotary-cutting tools are perfect for this process; you will need:

- rotary cutter
- cutting mat
- square ruler, larger in size than your block

1 When you're squaring up a block, you always square two adjacent edges at a time. So start by placing the block on the cutting mat with the two sides you want to square first to the bottom and the right.

Lay the ruler over the block, with the correct block measurement in the top left corner of the block (**a**). (For example: if you want to make a block 8in square, then the 8in measurement should be in the top left corner.) Adjust the ruler over the block until you judge that the block is centred and the edges of the block go slightly over the upper left corner measurement (**b**).

2 Using the rotary cutter, trim the right side of the block and then the bottom of the block (**c**); now the bottom right corner will be perfectly square.

3 Carefully turn the block round (or move your mat). Lay the ruler over the block again, with the correct block measurement in the top left corner of the block, and match this up exactly to the corner and the two straight edges you have just trimmed, as shown in the photograph overleaf (**d**).

◆ LESSON 4 ◆

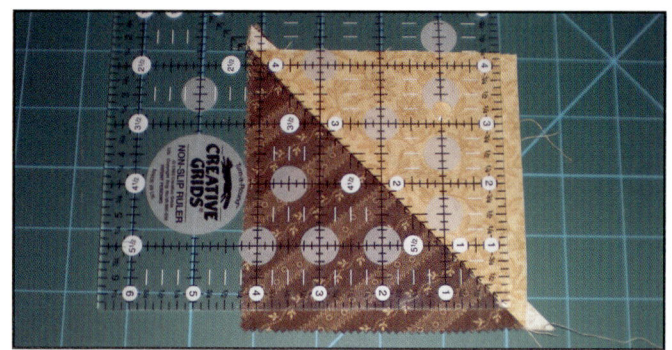

2 Place the ruler on top with the 4in measurement in the top left corner. Adjust the ruler over the block until the diagonal seam and the diagonal line on the ruler line up, and the edges of the block go slightly over the upper left corner measurement (**b**). Trim the right side and bottom of the block (**c**), then turn the block around and continue as above (**d** and **e**).

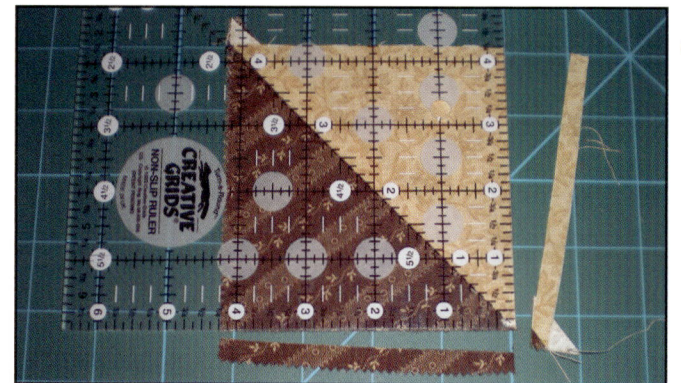

The other two edges (untrimmed) are now in the bottom right corner. Cut the right side and the bottom edge as before (**e**); you will now have a perfectly square 8in block.

◆ Squaring up a half-square triangle block

1 If you are squaring up a unit made up of two half-square triangles, it is important to use the diagonal line (45° angle) on your ruler/setting square. Before you trim any of the sides, lay the ruler on top of the block, aligning the diagonal line with the diagonal seam.

For example, if you wanted to make a block 4in square, then lay the block on the mat with the diagonal seam going from top left to bottom right (**a**).

Charming Triangles

Charming Triangles uses the quick-and-easy method of piecing half-square triangles; as you don't have to stitch along raw bias edges, the finished squares are more accurate in size. This quilt also gives you the opportunity to try several variations of a quilt layout.

Finished size: approximately 43in (109cm) square
Charm pack featured: Kansas Winter

You will need

◊ One charm pack (a total of thirty-two 5in squares)
◊ 70cm plain/tone-on-tone contrast fabric
◊ 50cm fabric for the outer border
◊ 40cm fabric for the binding
◊ 1.2m backing fabric
◊ Wadding, at least 1.2m square

Instructions

Use ¼in seams throughout

To assemble the central design

1 Cut four strips of the contrast fabric, each 5in wide x the width of the fabric. Sub-cut these strips into 5in squares to give you 32 plain square patches (**a**).

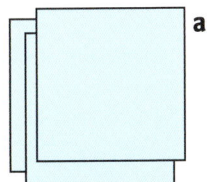

2 Follow the instructions on page 28 to mark a diagonal line on the back of each square, and to mark stitching lines ¼in on each side (**b**).

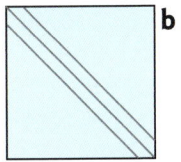

HINT
If you are sewing by machine and have a quarter inch foot, then you do not need to mark a sewing line.

3 Lay a plain square on top of each patterned square, right sides together. Sew along both stitching lines on all the squares (**c**), chain piecing if you're using a machine (see page 10). Using sharp scissors, or a rotary cutter, cut along the central diagonal line on each stitched square (**d**). Open out the squares and press the seam allowance on each towards the darker fabric; trim off the points (**e**). Each pair of squares will give you two plain/patterned half-square triangle blocks.

4 Make sure that the blocks are all the same size: they should measure around 4⅝in square, but it works well if you cut them all down to 4½in square (see the lesson on squaring up blocks on page 30).

5 Now arrange your squares into an 8 x 8 block pattern. There are many different ways in which to arrange these blocks to create different effects; the diagram (**f**) shows various arrangements.

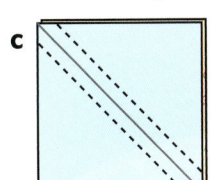 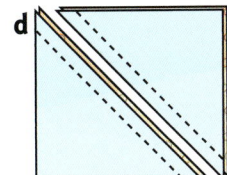 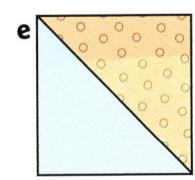

f

◆ PROJECT 4 ◆

For my quilt I created a 4 x 4 arrangement of the block shown (**g**).

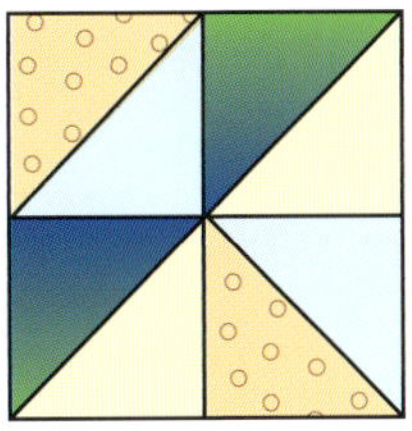

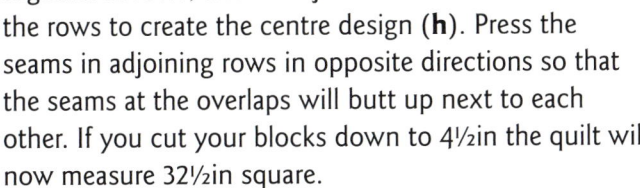

6 Once you have decided on a design, stitch the squares together in rows, and then join the rows to create the centre design (**h**). Press the seams in adjoining rows in opposite directions so that the seams at the overlaps will butt up next to each other. If you cut your blocks down to 4½in the quilt will now measure 32½in square.

To create the quilt top

7 Cut four border fabric strips each 5in wide x the width of the fabric. Trim two of these strips down to 32½in and stitch to the top and bottom of the pieced design. Trim the remaining two strips down to 41½in and stitch to the sides of the design to complete the quilt top (**i**).

Your quilt top is now complete; layer it with the wadding and backing fabric, then quilt and bind as you wish.

The Charming Triangles design in another colourscheme and layout

Wadding, Backing, Basting and Marking

Once you have made your quilt top you need to add wadding and backing before you start quilting. These three layers together are often referred to as a 'quilt sandwich.'

◆ Wadding

There are many different types of wadding (batting) on the market, ranging from 2oz polyester through to silk and wool. As with fabric, the better the quality of your wadding, the more enjoyable your project will be to quilt – and the better it will hang and wear. But, do consider how your quilt will be used: if it's for a child, and so will be frequently washed, then a polyester wadding may be better than a wool one. But if you like the slightly crinkled look of antique quilts, then choose a cotton wadding, as this is thinner and it will shrink slightly when washed. Or, for warmth, choose silk or wool wadding.

Wadding can be bought by the metre, or in pre-cut packs ranging from Craft Size (eg 36in square) to King Size (normally 120in square). If you are making several small projects from this book, then it may be more economical to buy a large bag of wadding rather than several smaller packs. Check the packaging – this will often give you information about the suitability of the wadding for hand or machine quilting, and how much it will shrink when washed.

Always take your wadding out of its packaging a few hours before you want to use it, to allow it time to 'breathe' and regain its shape if it has been crushed in packaging. Don't worry about the occasional 'hump and bump' in the wadding – these can be smoothed out as the quilt is tacked/basted and eventually quilted. If you decide to use a cotton or poly/cotton mix wadding, if you wish you can pre-wash it so that it's pre-shrunk before you layer it into your quilt.

It's useful to keep a snippet of the waddings you use in a notebook, with a note of the type and manufacturer, and how you found it to work with – then if you want to use it again you will know exactly what to buy!

◆ Backing fabric

The backing fabric for your quilt should be 100% cotton. If you are new to hand quilting then a 'busy' print for the backing is a good idea, as this hides uneven stitches! The piece of fabric for the backing needs to be at least 2in larger on all sides than the quilt top, as the quilt top may move and stretch slightly as you quilt. If you need to join lengths of fabric to make the backing, then cut off the selvedges and open out the seam to reduce bulk. The patterns in this book assume that the quilt will be quilted in one piece; there is also a technique called 'quilt as you go,' which enables you to quilt small sections and join them together once they are quilted (for more details on this technique, see Carolyn Forster's book *Quilting-on-the-Go*, also published by Teamwork Craftbooks). If you want to use 'quilt as you go' methods, then you will need extra backing fabric to allow for the extra seams.

◆ Layering, marking and tacking/basting

There are many different products on the market which you can use for marking out your quilting design; two different types of quilt marking pen are shown in the photograph. The marking method you choose will often depend on the colour(s) of the quilt top; you need to be able to see the quilting design clearly against the different fabrics. On light fabric, for example, use an ordinary pencil, a blue wash-out pen (the marks are removed with a light dab of clean water once the quilting is complete), or a purple evaporating pen (the marks disappear within about 24 hours). On dark fabric, use a white, silver or yellow pencil, a white marking pen, or chalk.

LESSON 5

1. Press the quilt top and mark your chosen quilting lines and patterns on the right side. Press the backing fabric too.

REMEMBER
If you mark your quilting lines with a wash-away pen, then don't iron over these lines – they will become permanent!

2. Cut a piece of wadding 3-4in larger than the quilt top; aim to have approximately 2in of wadding showing around the quilt top on all sides. Cut the backing to the same size as the wadding.

3. Lay the backing fabric right side down onto a flat surface – a large table or the floor. Keep this fabric as taut as possible, but do not stretch it: masking tape or soft furnishing clamps help to keep it in place. Lay the wadding on top, smoothing out any wrinkles with your hand, and working from the centre so that any excess wadding goes over the edges of the backing fabric.

REMEMBER
Do not press the wadding directly with an iron, especially if it contains polyester – it will melt!

4. Centre the quilt top over the backing and wadding to make the final layer of the sandwich. Starting at the centre and working towards the edges, smooth out any wrinkles in the top.

5. Using a long needle and contrasting thread, tack/baste the three layers of the quilt 'sandwich' together with large running stitches. Start from the centre of the quilt, and smooth the top and wadding as you baste – also check that the backing stays as flat as possible. Baste horizontally across the whole quilt, with rows of stitches about 2in apart; repeat with vertical stitches (**a**).

There are various other methods you can use to baste the layers of your quilt sandwich. One way is by using safety pins (the curved ones are easier to use), and this is a good idea if you are machine quilting. Keep the basting pins 6-8in apart (**b**).

Other basting options include:
- a basting 'gun' which secures the layers together with small plastic ties (**c**)
- basting spray which temporarily bonds the layers together
- fusible wadding

Remove the basting stitches, pins or plastic ties once the quilting is complete.

Charmed Broken Squares

A repeat block created from triangles is the star of this pretty lap quilt; the finished effect is a bit like small-paned windows set in a frame.

Finished size: approximately 41in (104cm) square
Charm pack featured: Blush

You will need

◇ One charm pack with at least thirty-six 5in squares
◇ 1 metre matching Moda Marble fabric for the sashing and outer border
◇ 20cm contrast fabric for the inner border
◇ 30cm fabric for the binding
◇ 1.1m backing fabric
◇ Wadding: crib size, or at least 45in square

Instructions

Use ¼in seams throughout

To make the basic block

1 Sort the charm pack squares into 36 pairs, making sure that the fabrics in each pair are a good contrast of colour and pattern (**a**).

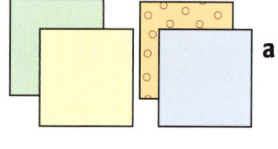

2 Choose one square from the first pair, and draw a diagonal pencil line across the back (**b**). Put the two squares right sides together and pin; sew a ¼in seam on each side of the drawn line (**c**). Cut along the drawn line (**d**), then open out the squares and press (**e**).

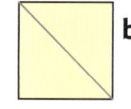 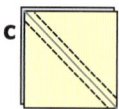
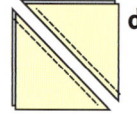 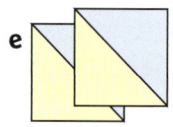

3 Mark, stitch and cut all the other pairs of squares in the same way (**f**), to produce 36 pieced units; follow the instructions on page 30 to square these up to 4½in.

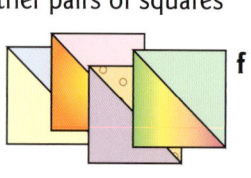

4 Sort the squares into nine groups of four, making sure that no fabric pattern is repeated in each set. Lay each set out so that the diagonal seams form a square 'on point' (**g**), then join

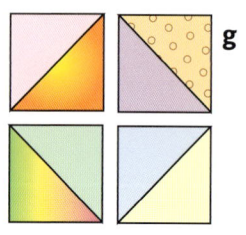

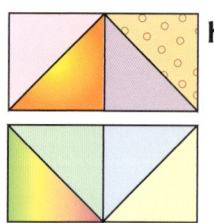 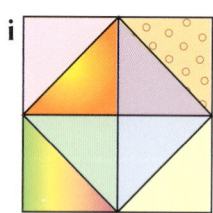

the squares in pairs (**h**). Finally, join the pairs to form a larger square (**i**), matching the central seams.

5 Make up all the groups of blocks in the same way to produce nine pieced squares. Follow the instructions on page 29 to trim the blocks to 8½in square.

To assemble the central design

6 From the sashing fabric, cut eight strips of fabric 2½in wide across the width of the fabric, and from these cut six 8½in lengths. Join three of the pieced squares into a row separated by sashing strips (**j**). Do the same with the other squares and sashing strips to create three rows.

7 Measure the length of the rows; they should be 28½in. If necessary, trim the rows slightly so that all three are the same length. Cut four of the sashing strips to the length of these

rows; use them to join the rows, plus one strip at the top and another at the bottom (**k**).

36

PROJECTS

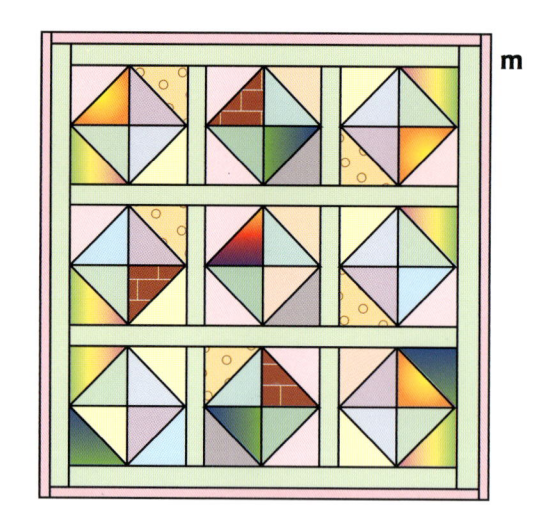

PROJECT

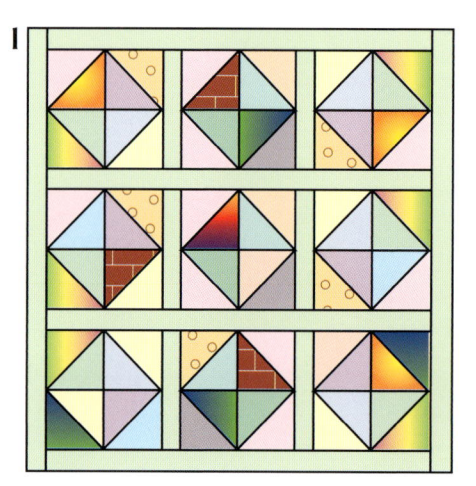

8 Measure the quilt top; it should now be 32½in x 28½in. Trim the final two sashing strips to 32½in, and stitch them down the sides of the design to create the central design (**l**).

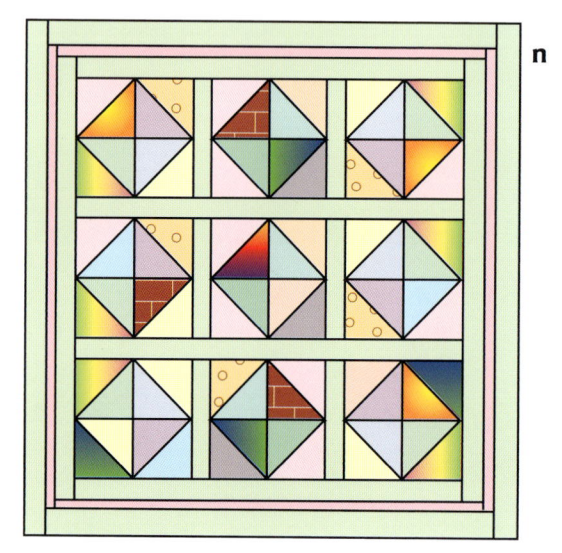

The Charmed Broken Squares design in a different colourway

To create the quilt top

9 Measure the central pieced design: it should be 32½in square. From the contrast fabric, cut two strips measuring 1½ x 32½in, and two measuring 1½ x 34½in. Stitch the shorter strips to the top and bottom of the quilt top, then add the longer ones to the sides to create the inner border (**m**). The design should now measure 33in square.

10 From the remaining sashing fabric, cut strips for the outer border; cut two strips measuring 3½ x 34½in, and two measuring 3½ x 40½in. Stitch the shorter strips to the top and bottom of the quilt top, then add the longer ones to the sides to create the outer border (**n**). The design will now be 40½in square.

Your quilt top is now complete; layer it with the wadding and backing fabric, then quilt and bind as you wish.

LESSON 6

Quilting

Quilting is the stitching that holds the three layers of a quilt together, but it also adds decoration and enhances the piecing in the blocks. Whether you are quilting by hand or machine, always begin quilting in the centre of the quilt and work outwards; this way the quilt stays nice and flat, and you avoid any puckers in the centre.

◆ Quilting by hand

If you're using a frame, secure the work in it so that it is firm but not taut – you need to be able to 'rock the needle' (see below) through all three layers. Using a single strand of quilting thread (18-24in long), make a knot in the end. Working from the back, insert the needle about 1in away from where you want to begin quilting. Run the needle through the wadding and bring it through to the front of the work at the start point. Give the thread a gentle tug, to pull the knot into the wadding (**a**).

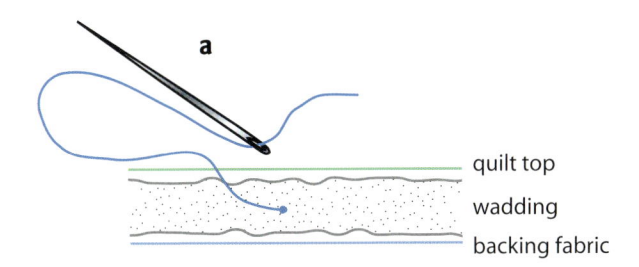

quilt top
wadding
backing fabric

The quilting stitch is a small running stitch which goes through all three layers – the quilt top, the wadding and the backing. Using a rocking motion with the needle, in and out of the work, aim to make three or four stitches (**b**) before you pull the thread through (**c**).

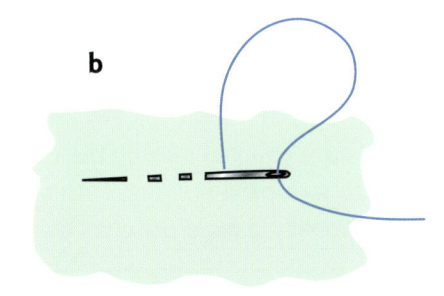

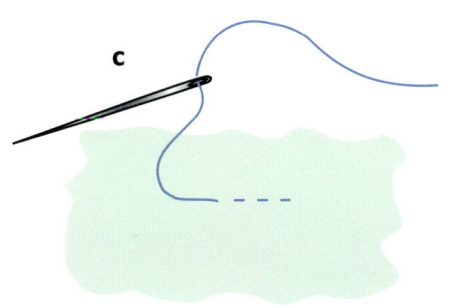

'In the ditch' quilting means that you sew along the seam line, and the stitches are less obvious than on other parts of the fabric patch. Don't try to quilt through folded seams as the bulk will make it difficult to push the needle through. If you quilt at least ¼in away from a seam then you should avoid the bulk of folded seam allowances.

When you are getting near to the end of the thread, or if you want to finish quilting, tie a knot in the thread close to the quilt top, and take the needle into the work right beside the thread. Pull this knot into the wadding. Bring the needle up about an inch from where the quilting finished (**d**) and cut off the excess thread. The photograph below shows an example of hand quilting.

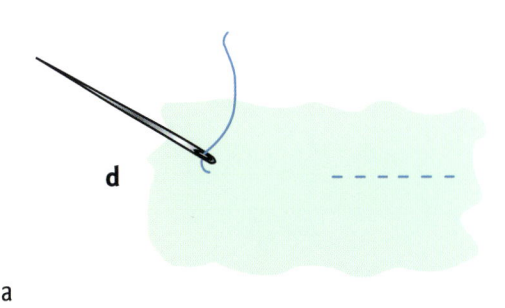

LESSON 6

◆ Quilting by machine

Although machine quilting is quicker than hand quilting, it takes a lot of practice to achieve good results. If you're a beginner, start with sewing straight lines only, and leave curves and free-motion quilting until you have more experience! For example, if you wanted to machine quilt the first project (Simple Charms), you could sew on the diagonal across the squares (**a**), and then quilt in the ditch along the border seams. You can also use fancy machine stitches for quilting if you wish. It is important to use a walking foot (**b**) on your machine when quilting – this attachment moves the top and bottom fabrics at the same rate, and so helps to prevent folds and puckers being formed in the backing fabric as the quilt moves under the machine.

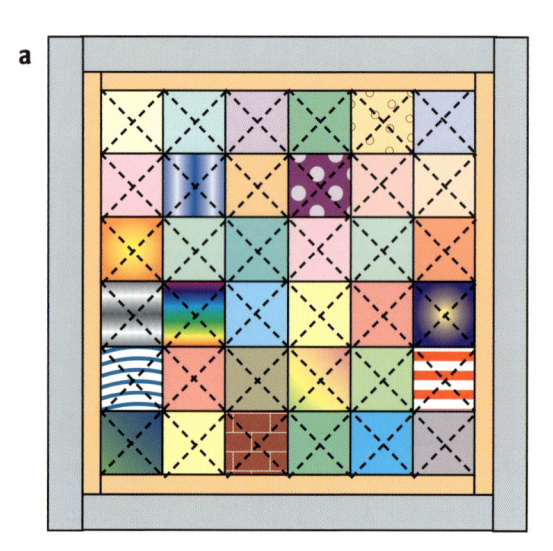

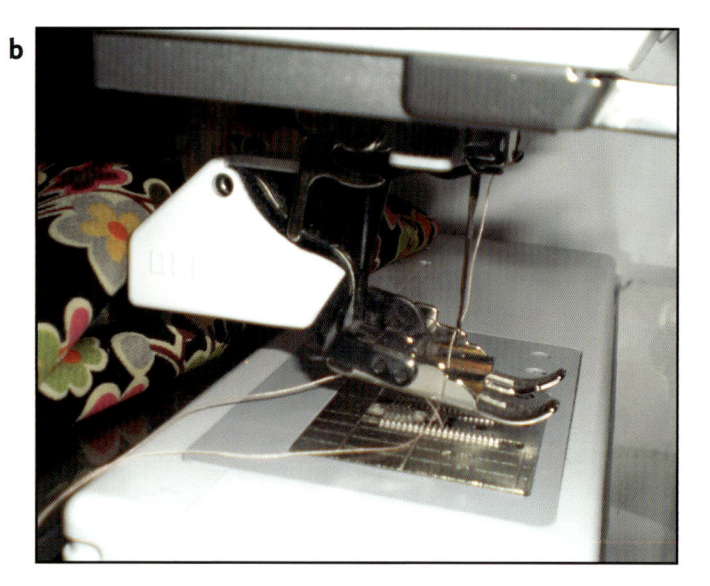

You can achieve more decorative quilting if you drop the 'feed dogs' on your machine. (These are the little ridged areas under the needle which move the fabric along at a regular speed.) Dropping the feed dogs allows you to stitch curves (**c**), and to create simple stipple or vermicelli quilting (**d**) – but if you're new to quilting, practise on spare fabric and wadding before you try the effect on your quilt. Once you're a bit more confident, you can create even more sophisticated designs with this kind of free machine quilting.

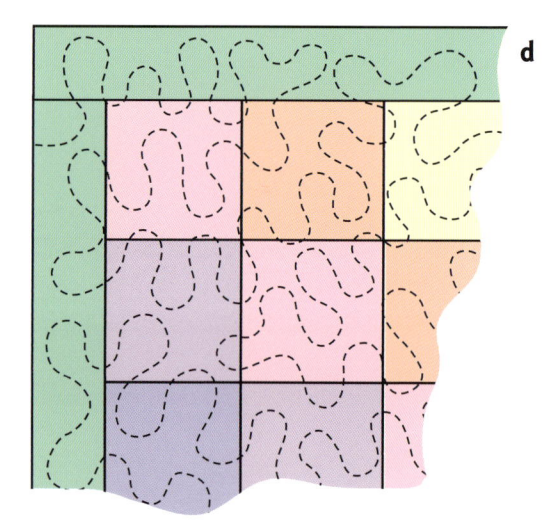

If you have enjoyed making the quilt top, but don't want to tackle the quilting, then your work can be professionally quilted using a long-arm machine (**e**).

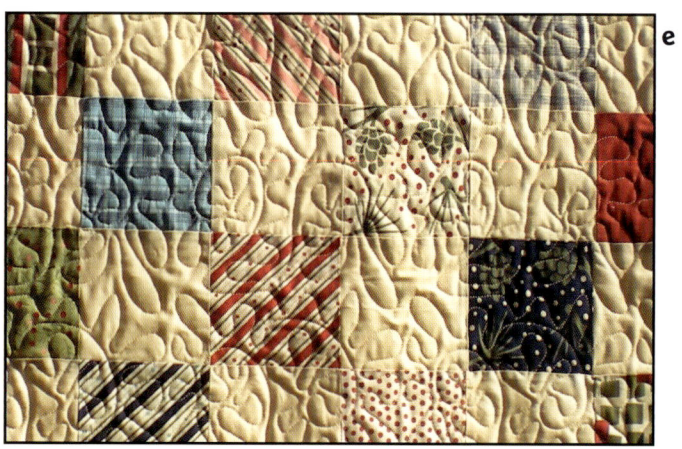

PROJECT 6

Star Charms

Use smaller squares in a contrast fabric to create stars that sparkle in a quilt of charm squares.

Finished size: approximately 40in (102cm) square
Charm pack featured: Evening Mist

You will need

- ◇ One charm pack (containing at least 36 5in squares)
- ◇ 40cm contrast fabric for the star points
- ◇ 25cm (thin quarter metre) fabric for the inner border; it works well if you use the same fabric that you choose for the star points
- ◇ 50cm fabric for the outer border
- ◇ 40cm fabric for the binding
- ◇ 1.2m backing fabric
- ◇ Wadding: crib size (or at least 45in/115cm square)

Instructions

Use ¼in seams throughout

To assemble the central design

1 Sort the charm pack squares into four groups of nine patches, each with a good mix of colours and patterns (**a**).

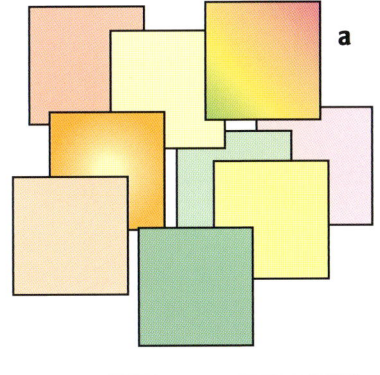

2 Using a rotary cutter and ruler, cut 48 2¾in squares from the contrast fabric. Draw a diagonal line on the back of each of these squares (**b**).

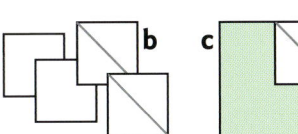

3 Take one of the centre 5in charm squares and four of the small (2¾in) contrast squares – these will make the four corner triangles of the square-in-a-square block. Place one of the small squares on the corner of the central square, right sides together (**c**).

4 Stitch along the diagonal line, then fold back the top contrast square and press, lining up the corner of this top square with the corner of the bottom larger square as you do so (**d**).

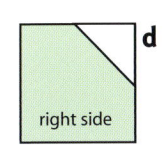

If it does not meet the corner of the square exactly, then unpick the stitching and resew. When you are happy with the placement, trim off the excess fabrics on the back of the work, ¼in away from the sewing line (**e**).

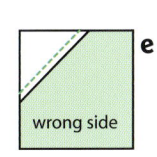

◇◇◇◇◇◇◇◇◇◇◇◇◇◇◇◇◇◇◇◇◇◇◇◇◇◇◇◇
NOTE
You can just trim off the contrast fabric at this stage, but it makes the seams thicker.
◇◇◇◇◇◇◇◇◇◇◇◇◇◇◇◇◇◇◇◇◇◇◇◇◇◇◇◇

5 Now take another of the small squares and place it on the next corner of the centre square (**f**). Once again, stitch along the diagonal line, check that the shape matches the corner of the centre square, press, and trim off the excess fabric (**g**). You will be sewing over the corner of the previous triangle: don't panic – this is correct!

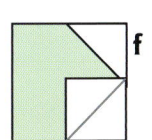

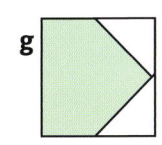

41

PROJECT 6

PROJECT 6

6 Use the same method to add two more small squares on the remaining corners of the charm patch to complete the central 5in square-in-a-square unit (**h**). Make a central unit in this way for each of your four groups of charm patches.

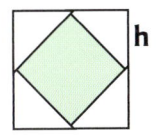

7 Take one of the sets of squares (one pieced square plus the remaining eight charm pack squares), and lay them out in a 3 x 3 arrangement with the pieced square in the middle (**i**).

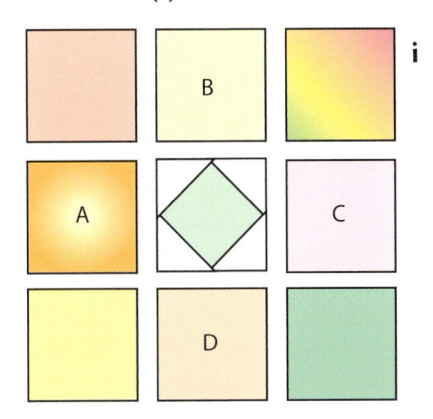

8 Using another two of the small contrast squares, and using the same method as above, sew star points onto two corners of square A as shown (**j**). Repeat this with squares B, C and D; when you lay all the squares out in position again, they now create a star design (**k**).

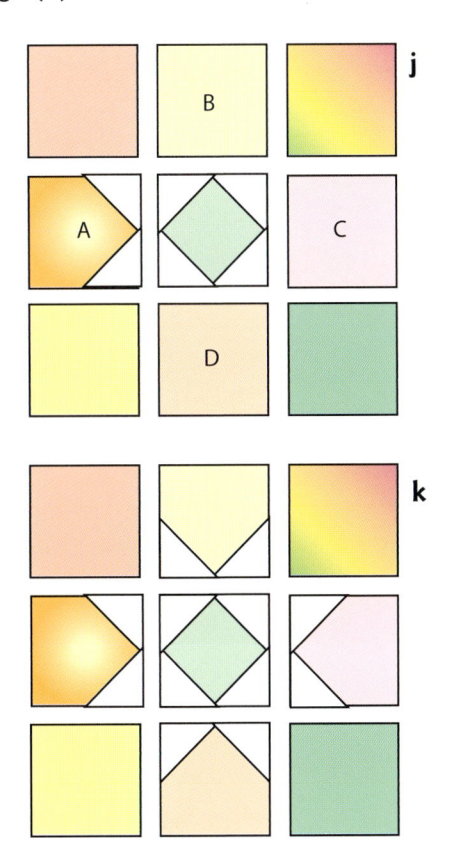

9 Stitch the top three squares together to make the top row and press the seams all in one direction. Stitch the next three squares together to make the centre row and press the seams in the opposite direction to the first row – then join the bottom row, pressing the seams in the same direction as the top row (**l**).

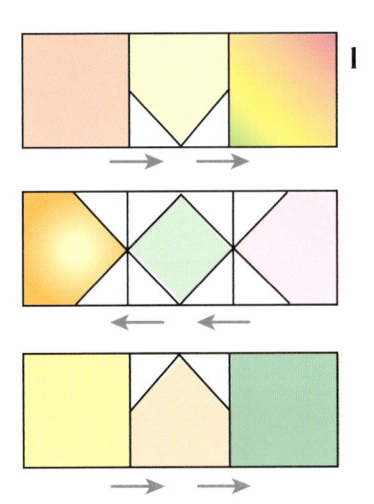

10 Pin the rows together, matching the corners, and butting together the seams at the overlap. Sew the rows together and press, to complete the star block (**m**).

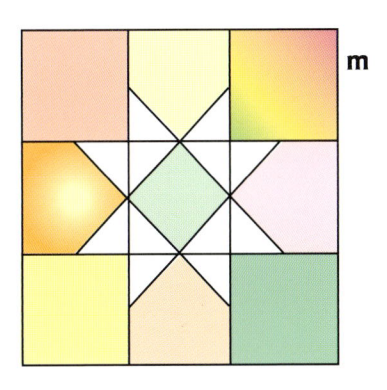

43

PROJECT 6

Repeat the process to make the other three stars, then join these star units to complete the central design (**n**). The quilt will measure 27½in square at this stage.

HINT
As you are joining the star blocks to assemble the central design, press the seams open where possible to reduce the bulk.

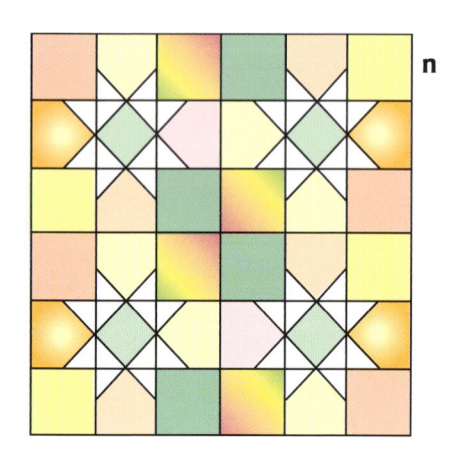

To create the quilt top

11 For the inner border, cut four strips measuring 2½in x the width of the fabric. Trim two of these strips to 27½in, and stitch to the top and bottom of the quilt. Trim the other two to 31½in, and sew to the sides of the quilt (**o**).

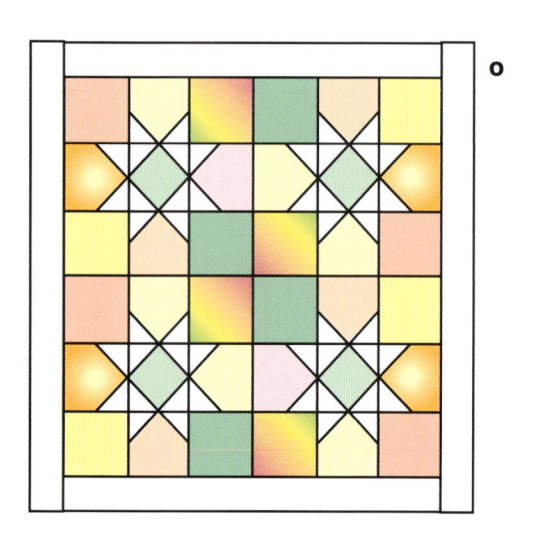

12 For the outer border, cut four strips each measuring 4½in x the width of the fabric. Trim two of these strips down to 31½in, and stitch to the top and bottom of the quilt. Trim the remaining strips down to 39½in, and stitch to the sides of the quilt (**p**).

Your quilt top is now complete; layer it with the wadding and backing fabric, then quilt and bind as you wish.

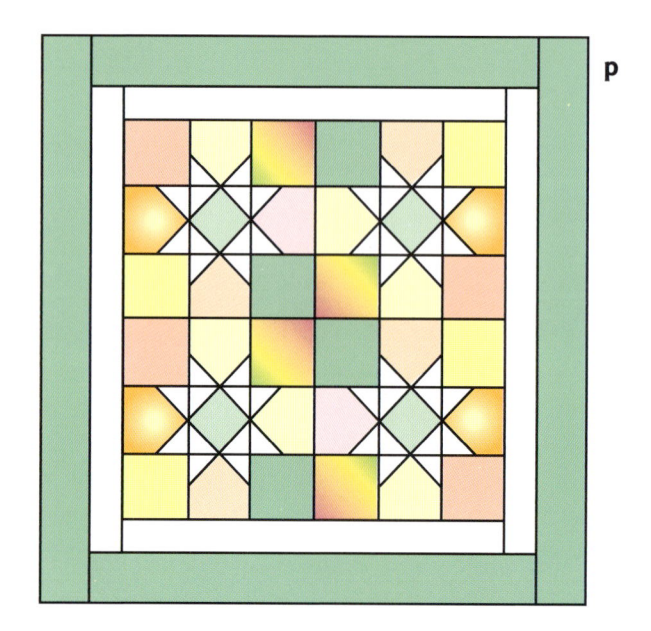

The Star Charms design in a different colourway

LESSON 7

Sewing Bias Seams, and Binding Quilts

◆ Sewing bias seams

When you are sewing bias seams it is important to pin the fabrics carefully, and to avoid stretching the fabric as you sew. If you are attaching sashing or borders to a bias edge, then cut the border fabric to the correct size and fit the bias edge to this.

In the section on fabrics on page 6, I talked about grain – the direction of threads running through the fabric. You probably remember that bias grain runs at 45° to the selvedges, and has the most amount of stretch. Stitching along the straight grain of fabric is easiest, as the fabric can't distort. Sometimes, though, the construction of a block means that you can't stitch along the straight grain – and sometimes, too, you want to make use of the 'stretch' afforded by stitching on the bias.

◆ Binding

Binding is the strip of fabric that's used to cover the raw edges of a quilt after it's quilted, and it is one of the last steps before you can finally say that the quilt is finished. Binding can be made from a fabric that is already in the quilt or you can choose something new. For all of the quilts in this book I have suggested cutting the binding strips 2½in wide – this gives a finished binding width of about ½in. You can make your finished binding narrower or wider if you prefer; just cut your strips narrower or wider accordingly. (You'll need a smaller or larger amount of binding fabric if you do this, don't forget.)

REMEMBER
Join the binding onto the quilt top before you trim away the excess wadding and backing; it's much easier to attach the binding this way, as otherwise the layers can move in relation to each other.

You need to cut enough strips to go all the way round the quilt, plus 6-8in overlap. Cut the strips on the straight grain of the fabric, and where possible across the full width of the fabric (approximately 44in) to minimise the number of joins. So, for example, if the quilt measures 36in square you will need to cut four strips across the width of the fabric. The binding is usually attached as one long strip to avoid bulky seams at the corners, and to enable you to make attractive mitred corners.

A quilt binding showing a diagonal seam

1 To create one long strip of binding fabric, join the ends of the strips using a diagonal seam. Lay the first binding strip right side up, and position the end of a second strip on top, right sides together and at a 90° angle (**a**). Mark a diagonal line from upper left to lower right and stitch along the line (**b**). Trim the excess fabric to ¼in away from the seam (**c**) and press the seam open (**d**), then add the other strips of binding fabric in the same way.

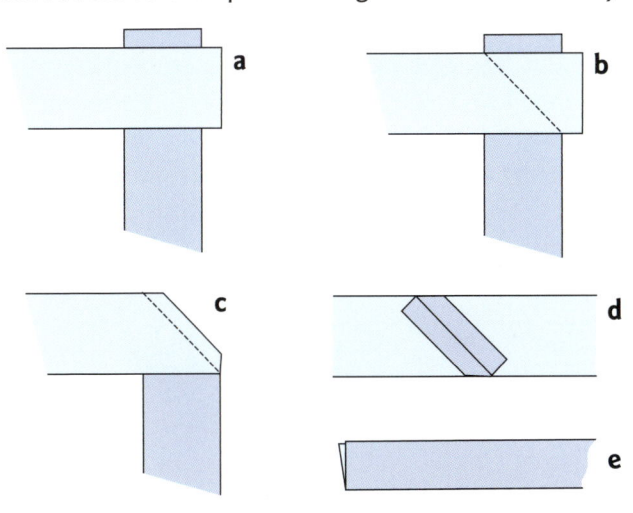

2 Fold and press the binding strip in half lengthways, with the wrong sides of fabric together (**e**).

REMEMBER
For this technique you fold the fabric wrong sides together.

LESSON 7

Starting approximately half-way along one of the sides of the quilt, align the raw edge of the binding with the edge of the quilt top. Leaving a free 'tail' of binding roughly 6in long, stitch through all layers, using a ¼in seam and stopping the stitching ¼in from the corner of the quilt (**f**). (If you are using a wider seam allowance, end the seam the same distance from the approaching quilt edge as the width of the seam allowance.) Backstitch at this point and cut the threads.

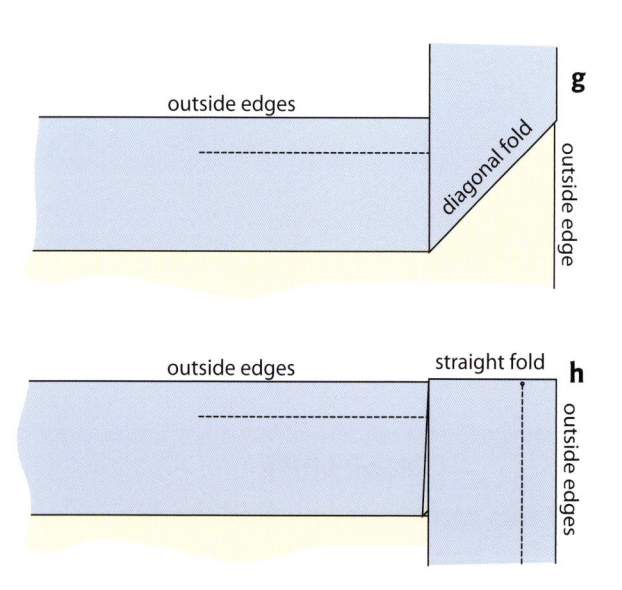

4 Continue sewing the binding around the quilt, mitring each corner as before. Stop stitching roughly 6in before the beginning of your original stitching line.

5 Lay the first free tail of the binding strip flat along the edge of the quilt top, then lay the other free end on top of it; carefully trim the binding strip so this overlap is the same width as the binding (**i**) – normally 2½in.

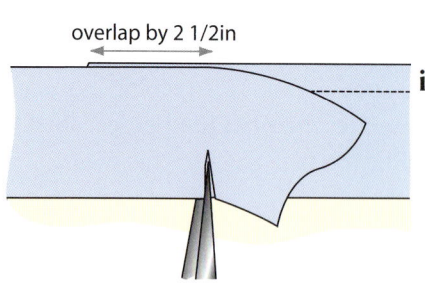

6 Unfold both ends of the binding strip and place them right sides together at 90°, as you did when joining the original binding strips. Mark a diagonal line as before, and then sew across this diagonal. Check that the binding fits correctly, repositioning and resewing the overlap if necessary. Then trim the excess, refold the binding in half, match it to the edge of the quilt top and stitch it in place (**j**).

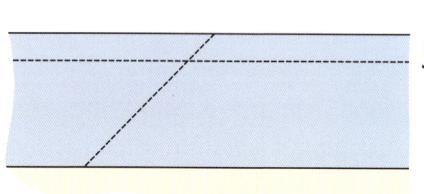

7 Trim the wadding and backing level with the raw edges of the quilt top and binding.

8 Fold the binding to the back of the quilt, covering the machine stitching, and blindstitch it in place. The mitres should fold neatly at the corners to form a 45° angle on the front and the back (**k**).

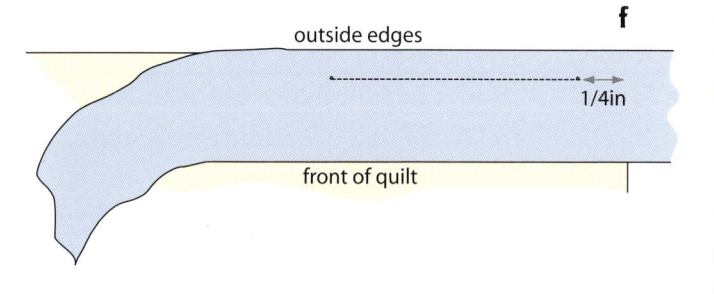

REMEMBER
If your machine has a walking foot, use it when you're attaching the binding – it helps to keep the layers from slipping.

3 Turn the quilt around to the next edge. To mitre the corner of the binding, fold the binding strip straight up at 90° to the edge you have just sewn (**g**); this creates a diagonal fold of binding in the corner. Finger-press this fold, and then bring the unsewn binding strip back down over itself, lining up the raw edges again (**h**). Begin stitching again, starting right at the folded edge of the binding and still using a ¼in seam.

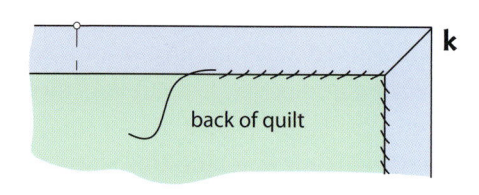

PROJECT 7

Charmed Twist

This attractive lap quilt/wallhanging is a quick and easy project suitable for quilters of all levels of experience; it's also a perfect showcase for all the different fabrics in a charm pack.

Finished size: approximately 39 x 50in (99 x 127cm)
Charm pack featured: Old Primrose Inn

You will need

- One charm pack (containing at least thirty 5in squares)
- 60cm background fabric (Moda Marbles work well)
- 25cm fabric for the inner border
- 50cm fabric for the outer border
- 40cm fabric for the binding
- 1.4m backing fabric
- Crib-size wadding (45 x 60in)

Instructions

Use ¼in seams throughout

To make the basic block

1 First of all, choose seven different 'feature' charm squares (ones with large or dramatic patterns on them), and set these aside (**a**). These are A units; you'll use these squares whole within the quilt design.

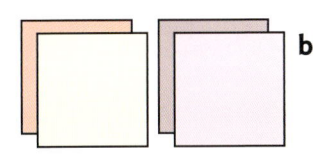

2 Put 22 other squares together in pairs; make sure that each pair features a mixture of colours and tones (**b**). Place each pair right sides together and stitch ¼in seams on opposite edges of the square (**c**).

3 Using a rotary cutter, cut the squares in half down the centre, keeping the cut parallel to the seams (**d**). Open the seamed patches and press them; from each pair of squares you have now created two rectangles measuring 4½ x 5in (**e**); these are B units.

4 Set aside 14 of these B units, and cut the remaining eight units in half, at 90° to the seams; this creates rectangles measuring 4½ x 2½in (**f**). Join these in pairs (once again mixing up the colours and tones as much as possible), to create four-patch C units measuring 4½in square (**g**).

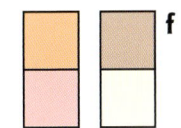

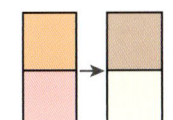

7 PROJECT 7

5 To piece the block, stitch the units in the following sequence:
- join one B unit to one A unit along the 5in side (**h**);
- join another B unit to one C unit, matching the seams as shown (**i**);
- join these patches together to make the final block (**j**).

Make a total of seven basic blocks this way.

To assemble the central design

6 Join the basic blocks to create two rows of two blocks and one row of three blocks as shown (**k**).

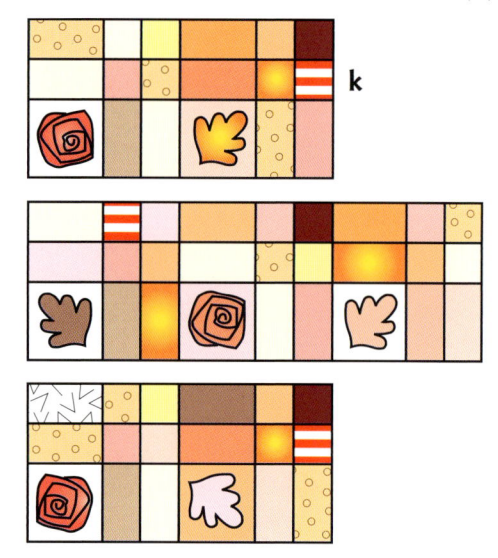

7 From the background fabric, cut three 13in squares (**l**). Cut two of these in half across the diagonal (**m**) to make the corner triangles of the quilt top – Y patches. Cut the remaining square into quarters across the diagonals (**n**); this will create the side triangles (X patches) – and you will have two spare.

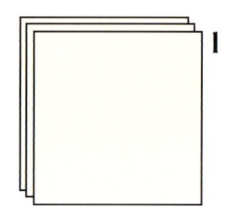

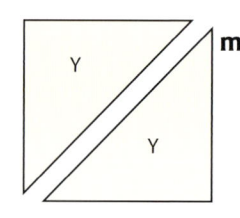

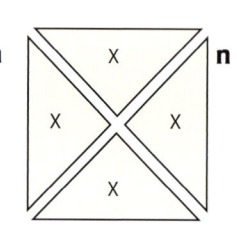

8 Join the X patches to the sides of the short rows as shown (**o**), then join the rows together in the layout shown (**p**).

9 Turn the pieced design so that it's 'on point' (at 45°), then join the larger Y triangles to the corners of the design as shown (**q**); if necessary, trim the X and Y patches so that the corners of the quilt top are completely square, leaving a ¼in seam allowance.

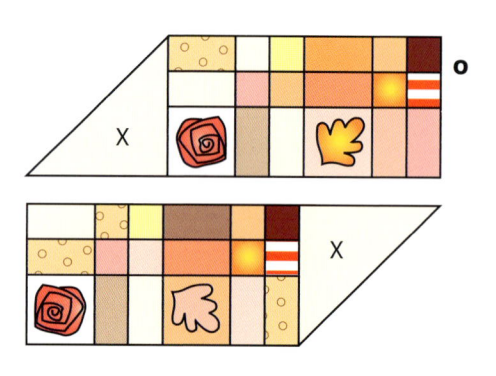

48

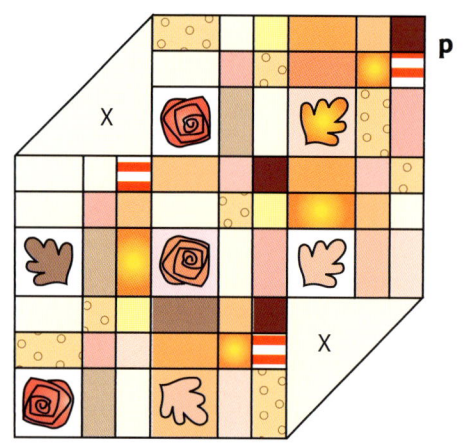

PROJECT 7

7 PROJECT 7

10 From background fabric, cut four strips measuring 2½in x the width of the fabric. Join two of these to the top and bottom edges of the design, then add the remaining strips to the sides (**r**).

To create the quilt top

11 For the inner border, cut four strips measuring 2in x the width of the fabric. Join these around the edges of the central design (**s**).

12 For the outer border, cut four strips measuring 4½in x the width of the fabric. Join these around the edges of the central design (**t**).

Your quilt top is now complete; layer it with wadding and backing fabric, then quilt and bind as you wish.

The Charmed Twist design in a different colourway

50

LESSON 8

Simple Appliqué

The word appliqué comes from the French, meaning 'application'; in quilting it means applying one piece of fabric onto a background fabric. Although in this lesson we'll have a look at several different methods of appliqué, we'll concentrate on needle-turn appliqué, as that's the method used for the project that follows. If you find that you enjoy appliqué, there are many patterns and books available which will give you the opportunity to expand your skills.

Examples of the appliqué motifs used in Project 8

◆ Different appliqué methods

Needle-turn appliqué

In this method, fabric shapes are cut out with a seam allowance and then applied to the background using hand stitching. The name 'needle-turn' derives from the fact that the seam allowance on the shape is turned under with the point of the needle as you work.

Machine appliqué

For this method, fabric pieces are cut out with a seam allowance and then applied to the background using machine stitching. The seam allowance is turned under and pinned before sewing, and the stitch used to secure the fabric pieces can be anything from a top-stitch, to a zigzag, to several so-called 'invisible' methods – you can find out more about all these methods in dedicated appliqué books.

Reverse appliqué

Reverse appliqué describes various methods which involve cutting shapes out of one layer of fabric to reveal a different fabric underneath. Sometimes the shapes are cut from the background fabric to reveal a secondary fabric; sometimes shapes are cut out of an appliqué motif to reveal the background fabric underneath. In some complex reverse appliqué techniques, several layers of fabric are cut back to different depths to reveal different colours.

Raw-edge appliqué

The raw edge in this title refers to the edge of the appliqué patch; the shapes are cut from fabric without adding a seam allowance or turning under the edges to neaten them. Hand or machine stitching can be used to attach the patches. When you're doing raw-edge appliqué it can often work well to stabilise the fabric with fusible interfacing to prevent the edges from fraying – however, occasionally the 'frayed-edge look' is what a particular design calls for!

◆ Appliqué basics

Preparing the background

You should always cut the background fabric slightly larger than the finished requirement: add at least an inch to both the length and the width. This is because the process of appliquéing pieces onto the background can pull the fabric up a little. Also, if you spend a long time working on a piece of appliqué, sometimes the edges of the background can begin to fray; once you have finished appliquéing the shapes you can cut the background to size and have nice clean edges.

Transferring the pattern to the background

First you need to find the centre of the background fabric. To do this, fold the fabric in half lengthways and widthways, and finger-press the folds. The point where the folds cross is the centre of the background fabric; mark this with a pin or a dot of chalk.

There are several ways to transfer the pattern to your background fabric. My two favourite methods are: marking the design directly onto the background fabric, and using an overlay.

Tracing the pattern onto the background

Either use a lightbox, or tape the pattern to a window on a sunny day, and centre the background fabric, right

LESSON 8

side up, over the pattern and secure it. (If you're using a window, tape down both the pattern and the background fabric.) Then trace the pattern onto the background fabric using a water-soluble pen or quilting pencil.

Using an overlay

Some people work this way all the time, but it's particularly useful if you are using a dark background fabric and it's difficult to trace through. For this method the pattern is traced onto a transparent or translucent material and placed over the background fabric, lining up the centre points; each appliqué piece is then positioned between the overlay and the background, using the traced design as a guide.

Clear plastic sheets work well for the overlay, and so does thin, non-woven interfacing. If you are using the interfacing, you can tack/baste the overlay to the top of the background and then flip it down and up as you position each appliqué shape.

◆ Preparing the appliqué pieces

Using templates

Create the template by tracing the relevant pattern pieces onto template plastic and cutting them out along the marked lines. Or, if you prefer to use card for your templates: trace or photocopy the shapes onto paper, stick the paper onto thin card, and cut out the template. Position each template on the right side of the appliqué fabric and trace around it using a water-soluble pen or a quilting pencil (**a**).

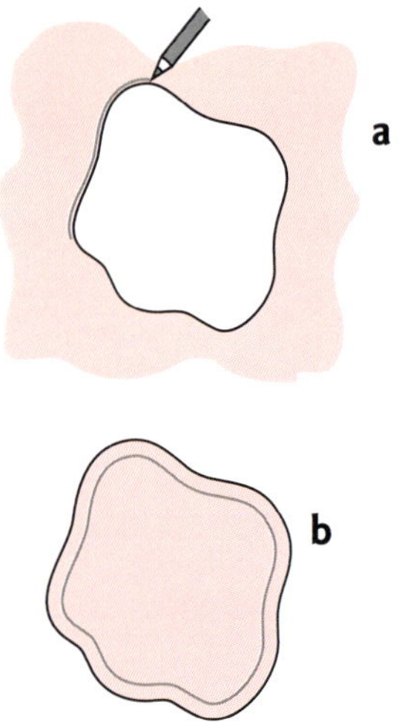

Cut out the shape, leaving a $1/8$-$1/4$in turning allowance around each shape (**b**). If you're a beginner, you'll find it easier to handle the appliqué pieces if they have the larger turning allowance, but this can create bulkiness on the underside of your appliqué. For this reason, cut as small a turning allowance as you find you can manipulate – don't make it too small, though, otherwise the stitches may pull out around corners.

Using freezer paper

Trace each pattern piece onto the paper (matt) side of the freezer paper and cut the shape out along the marked line (**a**). With a dry iron, press the freezer paper shape onto the right side of the fabric, shiny side down (**b**). Trace around the shape with either a water-soluble pen or quilting pencil, and cut out the shape, again leaving a $1/8$-$1/4$in turning allowance as above (**c**).

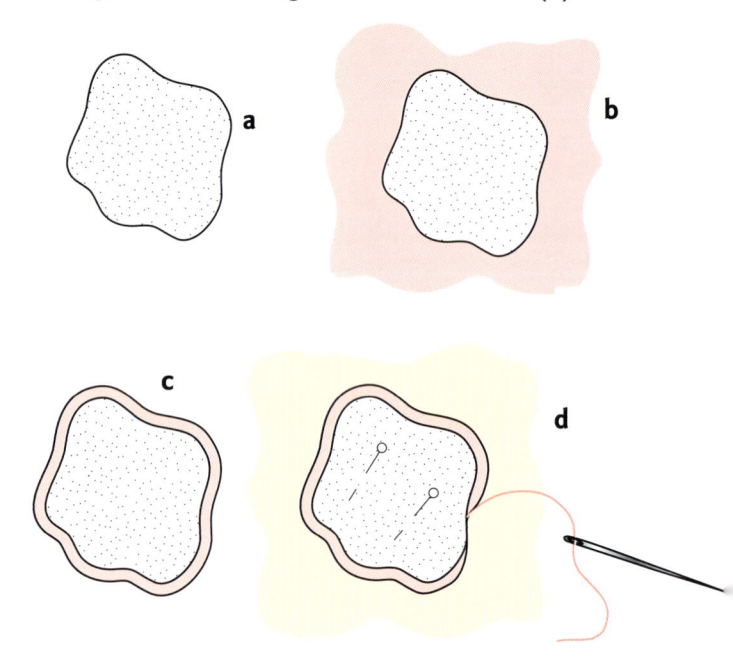

(If you prefer, instead of tracing around the shape and removing the freezer paper, you can appliqué the piece onto the background with the freezer paper still intact, folding under the edge as you go as shown in diagram **d**, and removing the paper when you have finished.)

Additionally, you can use the freezer paper shape on the inside of your appliqué piece. To use this method, first of all pin the freezer paper, shiny side up, to the wrong side of the fabric and cut out with a seam allowance as above. Then fold the seam allowances around the freezer paper, ironing as you go – the fabric will adhere to the freezer paper.

REMEMBER
Be careful only to iron the seam allowance; don't let the iron come into contact with the shiny side of the freezer paper.

Once all the edges are folded under, sew the appliqué patch to the background fabric, leaving the freezer paper shape in place inside the patch as you stitch. After you have stitched all the way around, you will need to cut a slit in the back of the background fabric, behind the appliqué piece, in order to pull out the freezer paper shape.

LESSON 8

HINT

Whichever method you choose, trace and cut the appliqué pieces on the bias of the fabric; this will make it much easier to turn under the spare fabric, and your appliqué shapes will be much less likely to fray.

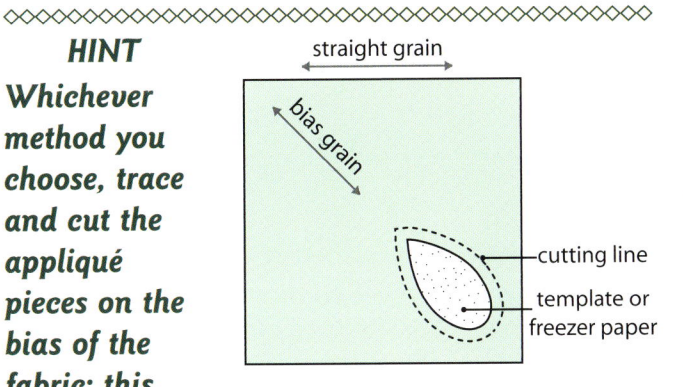

Getting ready to appliqué

- Choose threads that match the appliqué fabric, not the background. If you can't match the appliqué fabric directly, use a shade lighter than the fabric as darker threads are harder to hide.

- Use at least two pins on each appliqué patch to ensure that it can't move out of place while you stitch (**a**).

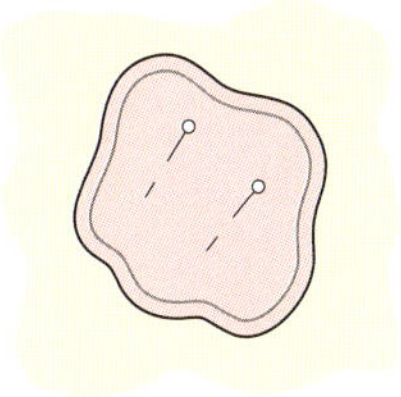

HINT

Appliqué pins are easier to use than normal sewing pins, as they are shorter and not so cumbersome.

- Always begin your appliqué by sewing any underlying pieces first – that is, any patch that is overlapped by another (**b**). Begin on a straight portion of the piece if possible, not on a point or corner. When you are matching two pieces together or overlapping one piece on another, start about an inch behind where two pieces meet or overlap.

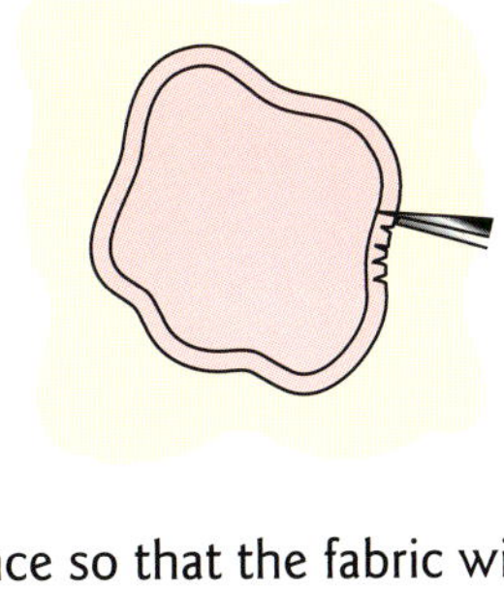

- On pattern pieces with inside curves, clip a small amount into the seam allowance so that the fabric will 'give' a little when it's turned under (**c**).

Doing needle-turn appliqué

1. Position an appliqué piece on the background and secure with pins.

2. Knot the thread and pull the needle up through the back of the appliqué piece on your drawn line or at the edge of your freezer paper. This will be the edge of the appliqué when the fabric is turned under so that the knot will be hidden inside the fabric (**a**).

REMEMBER

Begin stitching on a straight or gently curved edge, not a point or corner.

3. Take the needle back down through the background fabric exactly opposite the stitch on the appliqué shape (**b**), making sure that the stitch isn't slanting either forwards or backwards. Bringing the needle up from the wrong side, take a stitch through the background fabric and the edge of the appliqué piece, catching only a couple of threads of the appliqué fabric (**c**). Keep the stitches small, allowing about 1/8in between stitches. The thread will be visible on the wrong side of your work and almost invisible on the right side.

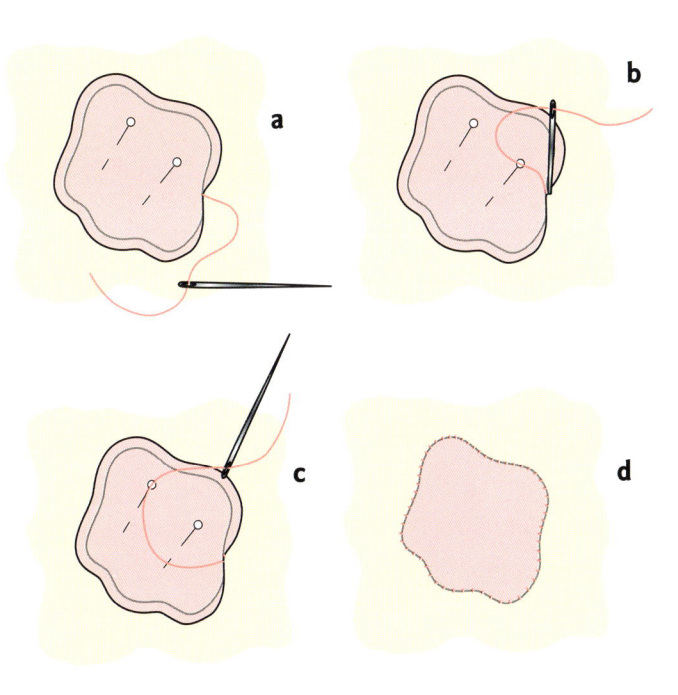

4. Continue stitching around the edge of the appliqué shape, turning under the seam allowance with the point of the needle as you work, and following the drawn line on the right side of the fabric (**d**).

PROJECT

PROJECT 8

Floating Flower Charms

If you're looking for an easy 'starter' appliqué quilt, this wall-hanging (made by Mimi Hollenbaugh) is ideal, as there are no sharp points or deep valleys in the appliqué shapes.

Finished size: 29 x 32in (74 x 82cm)
Charm pack featured: Mill House Inn

You will need

- One charm pack (containing at least thirty-nine 5in squares)
- Scrap of green fabric for the leaves
- 60cm background fabric
- 90cm backing fabric
- 30cm fabric for the binding
- 90cm wadding

Instructions

Use ¼in seams throughout

Preparation and cutting

1 Cut the background fabric so that it measures 22 x 30½in. Choose eleven charm squares from your set for the appliqué pieces. The sample pictured uses squares from a Mill House Inn pack in the following amounts:

- four of the red squares for the multi-petalled flowers
- three of the pink squares for the outside of the roses
- two of the maroon squares for the rose centres and the centre of the tulip
- one square of yellow for the insides of the roses and the centres of the petalled flowers
- one square of green for the tulip

The leaves are made from green scraps.

2 From the red squares, use templates A-F to cut three of each shape, mixing and matching the colours for each flower across the red fabrics.

From the pink squares, use template H to cut three shapes.

From the maroon squares, use template I to cut three shapes, and template L to cut one.

From the yellow square, use templates G and J to cut three of each shape.

From the green square, use template K to cut one shape.

From the green scraps, use template M to cut three shapes.

REMEMBER
Don't forget to add the turning allowance all round your appliqué shapes as you cut them out.

Sewing the appliqué

Most appliqué patterns have an overlay to show you where the pieces should be placed on the background. This pattern uses free-floating flowers, and is designed so that you can position the flowers where you wish. If you like the sample shown, use the photograph as a general guideline for positioning the pieces. Follow the instructions on page 53 (needle-turn appliqué) for appliquéing the shapes.

3 Sew the petals for the multi-petalled flowers first, pinning on the shapes you have cut from templates A-F. Make sure that all the petals are positioned so that all the points will be concealed once the centre is stitched on (**a**).

a

REMEMBER
Use at least two pins on each appliqué piece, and clip any inside curves.

Although there are sharp points on the inner ends of the petals, these will be hidden underneath the flower centres, so don't need to be folded under completely; begin stitching these pieces near the point on one side of the shape, and finish at the same position on the other side, leaving the tip of the point unsewn (**b**).

b — start stitching here

55

PROJECT 8

(The centre shape – cut from template G – will be stitched on later.)

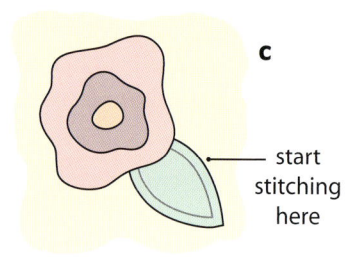

4 Pin and sew the leaves next (cut from template M). Start sewing about half-way up the leaf (**c**) and stitch all the way up to the point. When you are turning the point, you will need to make two folds in the fabric. First, clip off any extra turning allowance that shows behind appliqué piece (**d**). Then, pull the shape open so that you can see the underside of the leaf piece and fold the tip of the fabric down into a 'dog ear' (**e**), pulling the needle and thread to make sure the point of the leaf is fully sharp. Finally, fold under the fabric that is on the other side of the point and continue sewing (**f**). Make sure that you work the stitches close to each other on each side of the point, to ensure that none of the folded fabric peeks out.

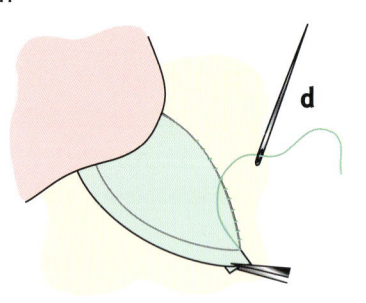

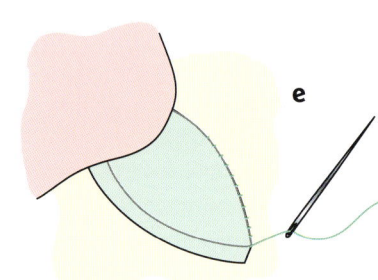

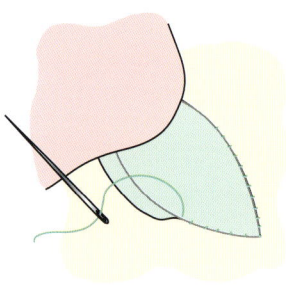

5 Pin and sew the two outer layers of the roses (templates H and I) next, followed by the tulip (templates K and L).

6 Finally, sew the centres of the multi-petalled flowers and roses (templates G and J). The flower centres on this quilt have been deliberately drawn in a slightly uneven oval shape, to make them easier to appliqué. However, if you would like to make perfect circles for the centres, use the following method:

*Cut a template the size of your finished circle in template plastic or card. From the appliqué fabric, cut a circle quite a bit larger than the template (**g**). Position the fabric circle over the template, then work running stitches around the edge of the fabric behind the template (**h**); pull the gathering stitches tight (**i**). Iron the circle flat, then loosen the stitches carefully and remove the template. You now have a perfect fabric circle, ready to appliqué in the centre of your flower (**j**). (You can trim the seam now, before stitching, if it turns out to be too bulky.)*

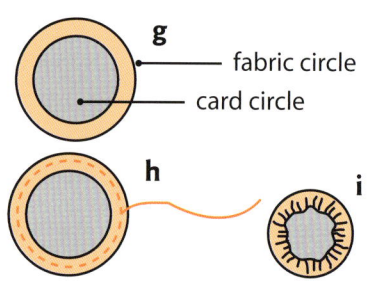

7 Now that your appliqué is complete, cut the background fabric to the finished size of 21 x 29½in.

Assembling the quilt top

8 Select 28 charm squares for your border and place them into pairs (this will give you a total of 14 pairs). Follow the instructions on page 28 to stitch these pairs into new squares formed of half-square triangles (**k**).

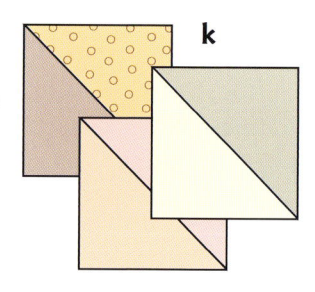

56

PROJECT 8

9 Stitch four rows of seven squares together to form the borders of the hanging (**l**); look carefully at the diagram to ensure that you join the squares with the

l

triangles going the correct way in each border. Stitch the borders onto the left and right sides of the appliqué design first (**m**), followed by the top and bottom (**n**).

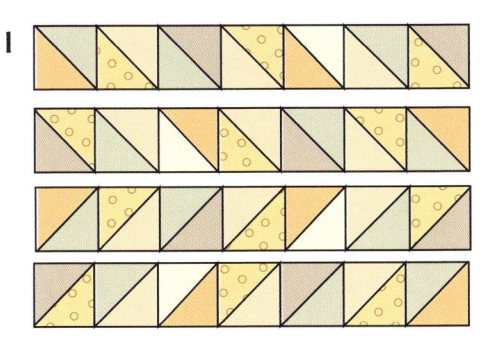

m

n

Your quilt top is now complete; layer it with wadding and backing fabric, then quilt and bind as you wish.

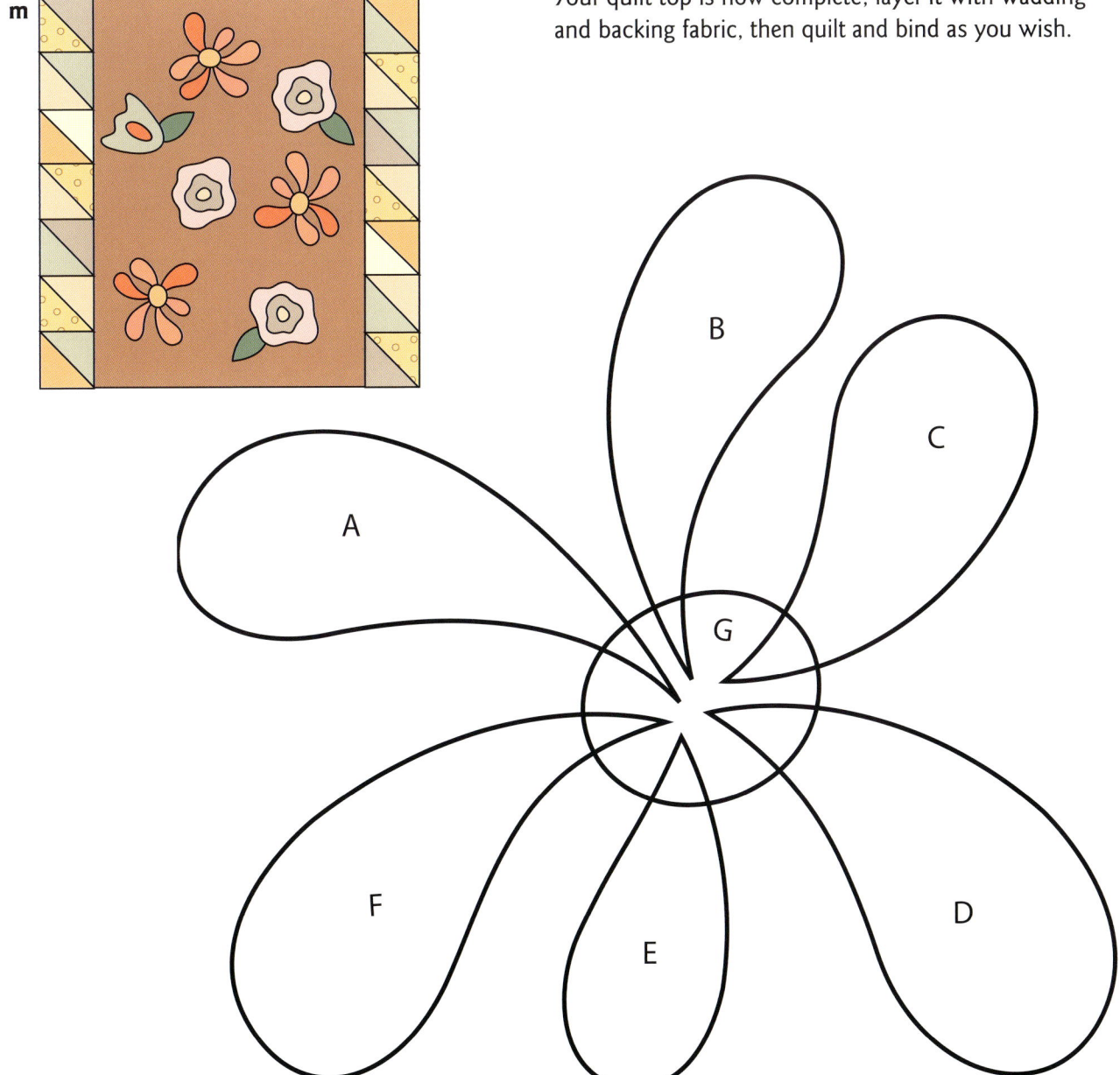

A B C D E F G

57

PROJECT 8

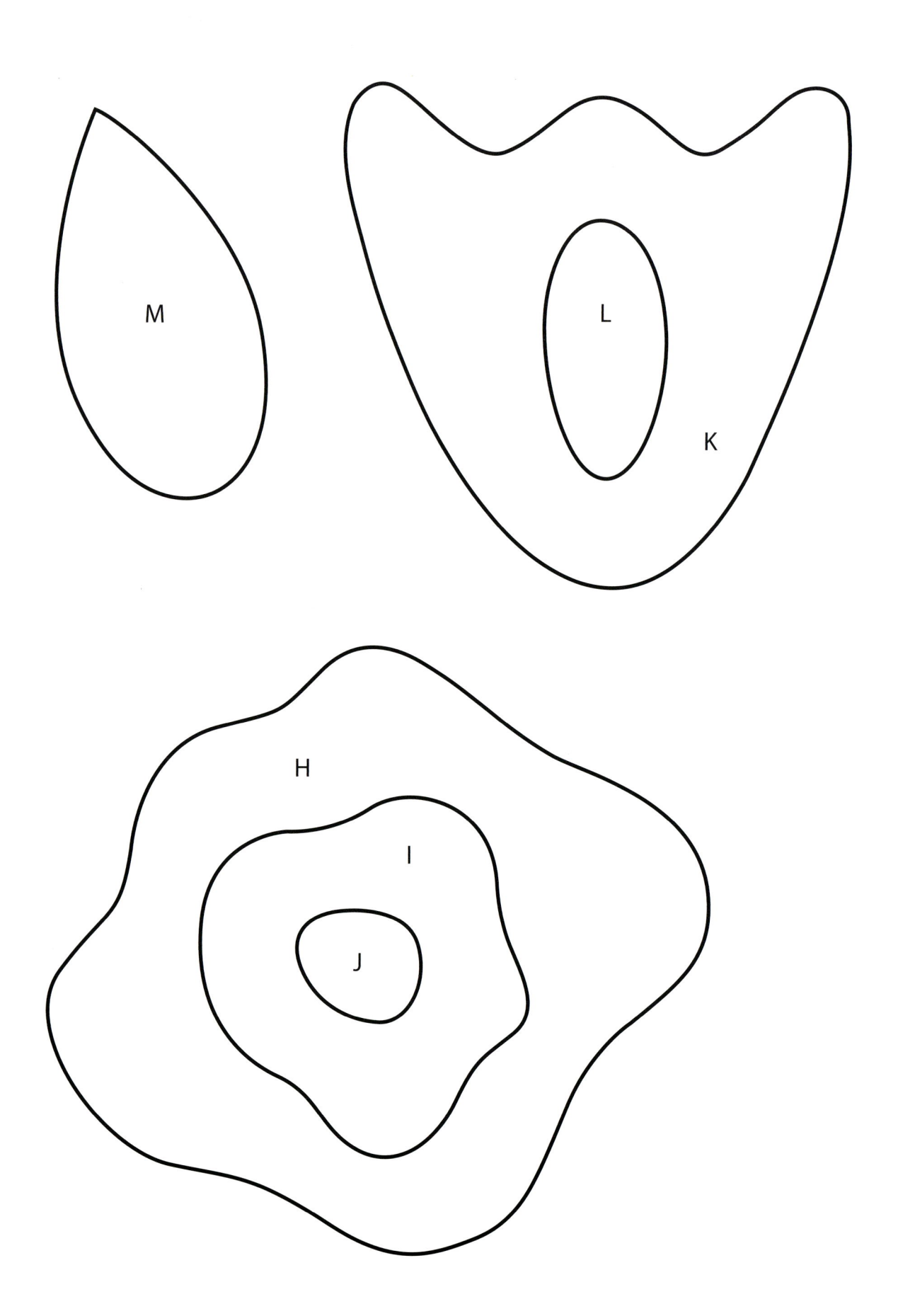

M

L

K

H

I

J

LESSON 9

Choosing Fabrics

Choosing your fabrics is often the most difficult part of making a quilt! Not only is there a vast range of fabric available in every conceivable colour, but you will also discover a multitude of fabric 'styles,' from bright spots to calm taupe prints. Making a quilt with a charm pack, or another pre-cut selection such a Jelly Roll or a Layer Cake, takes away some of the problems of fabric choice, as Moda have selected fabrics that are meant to go together.

Open up one of these pre-cut packs, and you will notice that there are several colours in the batch of fabrics, and also a variety of print sizes and styles – but the whole group has a sense of unity, as the same colours are combined in several designs, and the patterns have a common style. Even if you use a pre-cut pack, though, remember that you still have to think about borders, contrast fabrics and backing.

If you are choosing fabric from scratch, then first of all find one fabric you like – a 'focus fabric' – and add to it; these tips may help.

- Pick fabrics that will either blend with each other (blues going into purples, for instance), or which contrast sharply (for example, red and green)
- Lots of small prints create a soft look (for instance, if you use collections of 1930s fabrics or prints), whereas lots of large prints mixed together generate excitement (think Kaffe Fassett quilts), and plain colours together look bold and strong (as in Amish quilts). Most quilts include a variety of print size and texture in the fabrics.
- Tone-on-tone prints (for instance a mid-cream flower print on a pale cream background, or blue dots on a blue background) are good for backgrounds, sashing, and in blocks where busy prints need to be broken up.

◆ **The colour wheel**

The colour wheel is a useful tool for identifying which fabric colours to put together

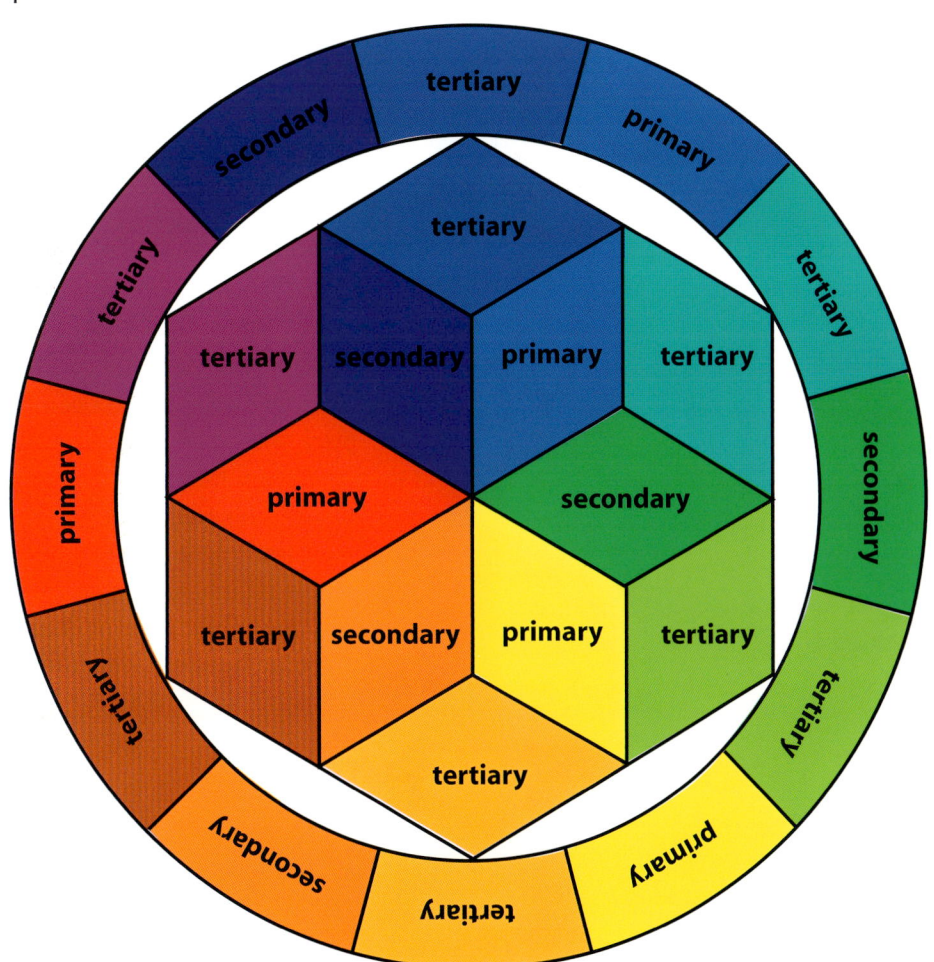

LESSON 9

primary colours

secondary colours

tertiary colours

neutrals

complementary pairs

a selection of colours which blend around the colour wheel

a similar selection from a different section of the colour wheel

a selection of blending colours plus a complementary accent colour

- Warm colours are on the left of this colour wheel, and cool colours on the right.
- The three primary colours (red, blue, yellow) are the key colours: they cannot be made from any other colour.
- If you mix equal amounts of any two primary colours, you create what are known as the secondary colours: purple, green and orange.

    red + yellow = orange
    red + blue = purple
    blue + yellow = green

- If you mix a primary with a secondary colour, in a ratio of 2:1, you produce a tertiary colour – for instance red-orange, blue-green etc.
- Neutrals, or non-colours, don't appear on the colour wheel: these include black, grey and white – and sometimes brown and beige are considered neutrals. These neutrals all go together and can be layered and mixed and matched. No neutral colour will try to dominate over another.
- Fabrics in colours next to one another on the wheel will blend into each other – for instance blues blend into greens. For a contrast that works well, use fabrics in colours which are opposite each other on the wheel: red complements green, blue complements orange, and purple complements yellow. Not surprisingly, these colour pairs are known as complementary colours.
- An accent colour is one used in quite small quantities to lift a colour scheme, and it should ideally be in a complementary colour. It works best if it's a bright, vibrant colour. Accent colours are perfect if you're scared of using strong colour – simply add a splash of an accent colour in small sections of the blocks/quilt.

◆ Value and intensity

Any colour also has value and intensity. Value is the lightness or darkness of a colour – for instance, burgundy is a dark value of red. Intensity refers to the saturation or brightness of a colour: for example, pillar-box red is an intense colour, a delicate pink is a pale colour.

There are filters available which will help you to look at fabrics to judge their value, but use them with caution as different filter colours display warm and cool fabrics in varying ways. It can help to use a scanner or copier to make black and white photocopies of your fabrics and then sort them for colour value. Also, look at fabrics from a distance: this helps you to see which fabrics stand out or blend together. Use a spy-hole magnifying glass (available from hardware shops – these are the little lenses you can put in front doors to see who's outside) to get a 'far away' view of your fabrics.

To help you to see how a fabric will look in your quilt, try viewing it 'through a window.' Make a window template by cutting a hole in a piece of card; make the hole the same size and shape as the finished patch in your quilt. When you look at the fabric through the window template you will have a better idea about how the fabric will look in your quilt.

PROJECT 9

Basket of Charms

More challenging piecing this time – but it all comes from your charm squares! Once you've finished the four basket blocks, try out the effects of different layouts (see page 65) before you sew the blocks together.

I've used cream fabric as the background, which shows off all the coloured fabrics, but you could use any plain colour which is a good contrast to your other fabrics.

Finished size: approximately 54in (137cm) square
Charm pack featured: Oz

You will need

- ◇ 1 charm pack with at least 40 5in squares
- ◇ 1m cream fabric
- ◇ 15cm co-ordinating fabric for the small triangles along the tops of the baskets (fabric A)
- ◇ 25cm contrast fabric for the large triangle in the top of each basket (fabric B)
- ◇ 40cm fabric for border 1
- ◇ 70cm fabric for border 2
- ◇ 40cm fabric for the binding
- ◇ 58in square wadding
- ◇ 3m backing fabric

Instructions

Use ¼in seams throughout

To make the basket block

1 Cut the plain fabric into the following sizes:

- four 4½in squares
- twelve 5in squares
- eight 4½ x 12½in rectangles
- two 8⅞in squares, cut along one diagonal to create four triangles

Take the twelve 5in squares, and on the back draw in one diagonal in pencil.

2 From fabric A cut four 5in squares (A squares). From the same fabric cut four 4⅞in squares, then sub-cut these four squares along one diagonal to create triangles (A triangles). You now have four squares and eight triangles in fabric A.

HINT
You'll find it helpful to mark the different squares and triangles with their relevant letters – write the numbers on scraps of paper and pin them to each pile of fabric patches.

Take four of the cream 5in squares and put them in pairs with the four A squares, right sides together. Follow the instructions on page 28 to make these into half-square triangle units, and cut these units down to 4½in square. You now have eight square A units (**a**).

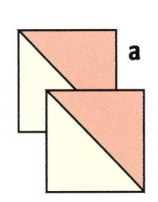

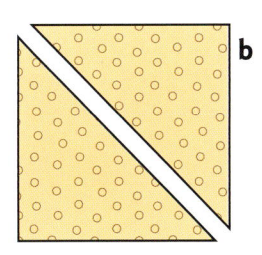

3 Cut fabric B into two 8⅞in squares, then cut each of these along one diagonal to create four large B triangles (**b**).

PROJECT 9

4 Sort the charm pack into:

- four squares for the 'feet' of the basket. Cut each of these down to 4⅞in squares, and then cut each of these new squares along one diagonal to make eight C triangles (**c**).
- eight squares for the flower points (D squares).
- twenty four squares grouped into twelve pairs, each pair featuring a patterned square (E squares) and a tone-on-tone or small-patterned square (F squares).

5 Put the remaining eight cream squares right sides together with the eight D squares. Follow the instructions on page 28 to join these into half-square triangle units, and trim these units down to 4½in square. You now have eight D units (**d**).

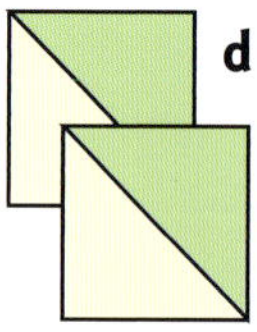

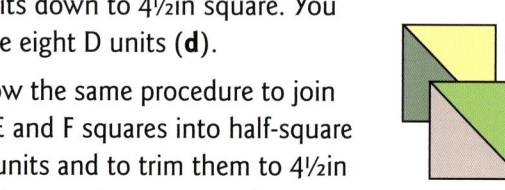

6 Follow the same procedure to join the E and F squares into half-square triangle units and to trim them to 4½in square. You now have twenty-four EF units (**e**); you will need six per basket block.

HINT
Throughout the assembly of the blocks, look at the diagrams carefully to ensure that you join the patches correctly.

7 Take four D units, one 4½in cream square and one large B triangle. Join two of the D units as shown (**f**), then stitch this new piece to the short, left-hand side of the large triangle as shown (**g**). Join the cream square and the other two D units into a row as shown (**h**), then join this row to the top of the first shape (**i**).

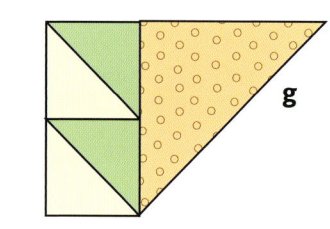

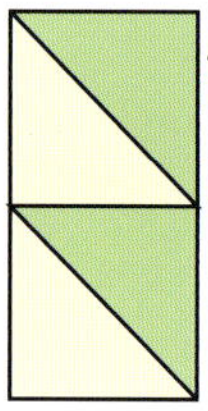

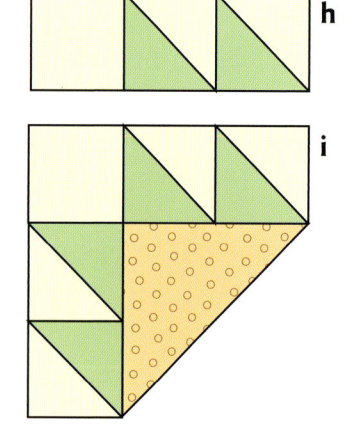

8 Take one of the square EF units and two of the small A triangles and sew them together as shown (**j**). Join this new unit to the one you made in step 7, to create a square (**k**).

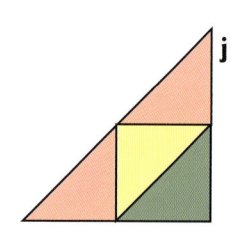

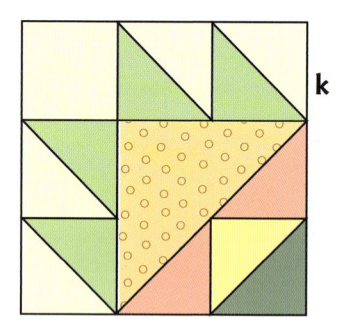

9 Take one square A unit and two EF units and join them in a row as shown (**l**). Stitch this to the bottom of the unit you made in step 8 (**m**).

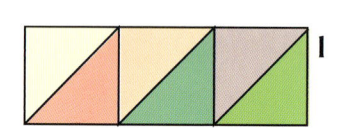

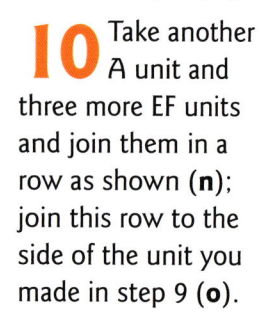

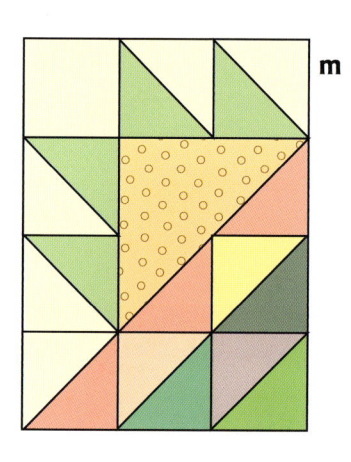

10 Take another A unit and three more EF units and join them in a row as shown (**n**); join this row to the side of the unit you made in step 9 (**o**).

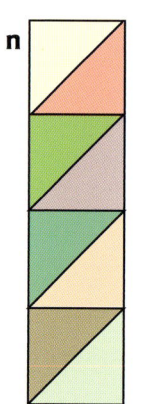

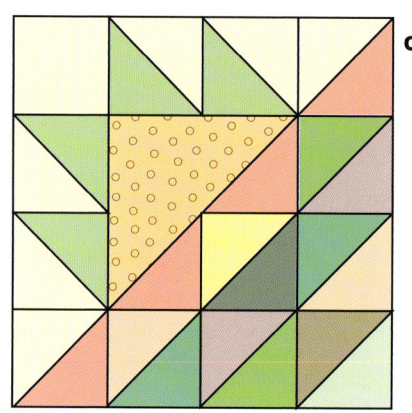

11 Pick two of the C triangles you've cut for the 'feet' of the basket, and join one to each end of a cream rectangle as shown (**p**, overleaf); sew these onto the sides of the central unit (**q**).

PROJECT 9

PROJECT 9

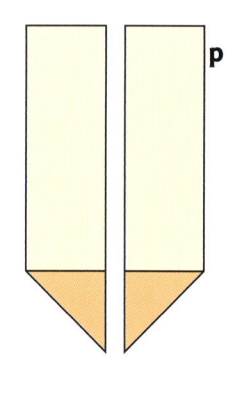

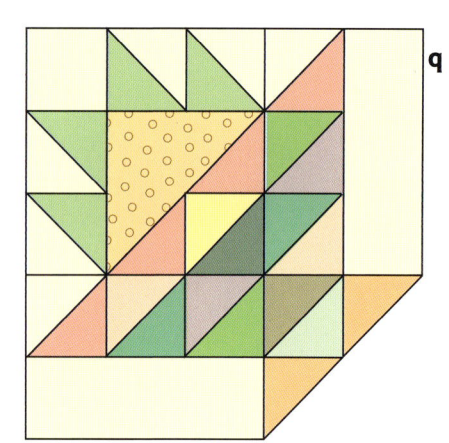

12 Finally, sew on a large cream triangle to complete the design (**r**); the block should measure 20½in square. Make three more blocks in the same way.

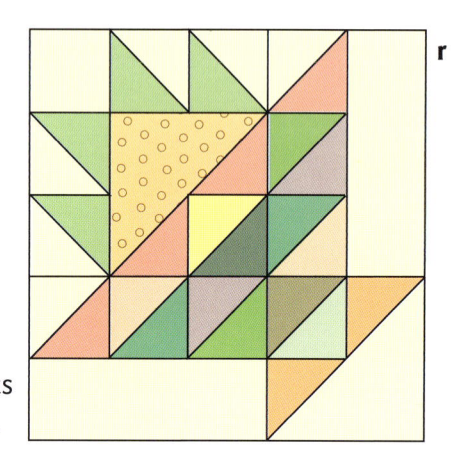

Assembling the quilt top

13 Join the four blocks; the diagrams opposite show different ways in which you can arrange the basket blocks. The layout I have used creates a large central diamond in the cream fabric – ideal for a single quilting motif.

14 Cut the Border 1 fabric into five strips, each measuring 2½in x the width of the fabric. Cut two of these down to 40½in and stitch them to the top and bottom of the quilt. Join the other three strips, then cut this new length down to make two strips 44½in long; sew to the sides of the quilt (**s**).

15 Cut the Border 2 fabric into five strips each measuring 5in x the width of the fabric, and join these strips into one length. From this new length cut two 44½in strips and two 53½in strips; sew the shorter ones to the top and bottom of the quilt, then join the remaining strips to the sides (**t**).

Your quilt top is now complete; layer it with wadding and backing fabric, then quilt and bind as you wish.

The Basket of Charms design in a different colourway

PROJECT 9

65

LESSON 10

Making Bow Tie Blocks

Another cunning way you can use charm packs is to create blocks in the pattern known as Bow Tie. This unusual design is a mixture of piecing and fabric folding, and creates a slightly 3D effect which looks very striking on the finished quilt.

HINT
You might like to practise making the block with full-size charm squares (ie, using five 5in squares for each block) to get the hang of the technique before you make the quilt in project 10, which uses smaller squares.

1 To make a Bow Tie block you need three squares of the same pattern or colour, and two background squares (**a**).

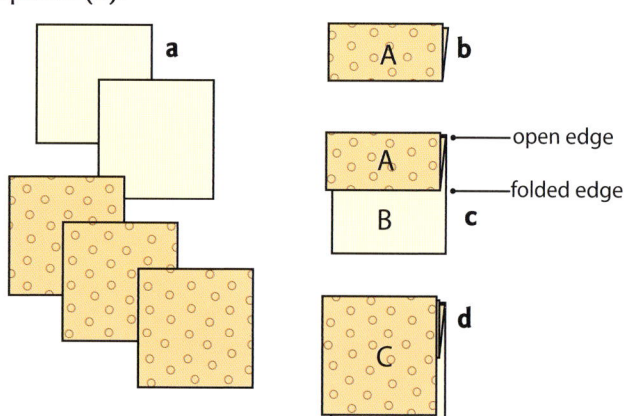

2 Take one of the patterned squares (square A) and fold it in half horizontally (**b**). Lay a background square (square B) on the table, right side up, and place the folded square A on top, with the long open edge at the top (**c**). Finally, place another patterned square (square C) on top of the other pieces, right side down (**d**).

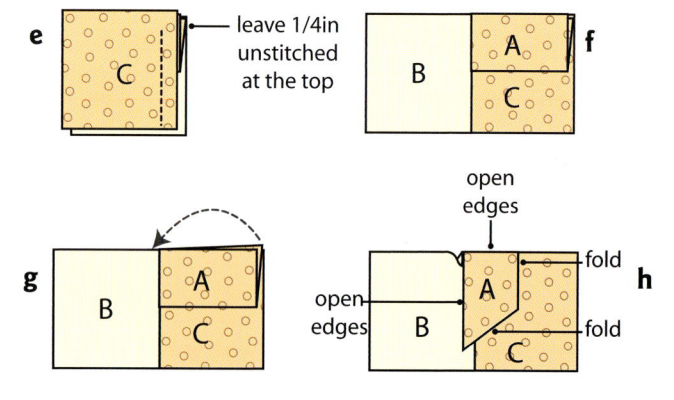

3 Stitch down the right-hand side of the stack of fabrics, stopping ¼in from the top (**e**). Open out the piece (**f**); take the back right-hand corner of square A, and bring it to the centre line at the top (**g** and **h**), lining up the edges as shown; make sure that the very tip of that fabric corner is tucked right into the centre of the shape.

4 Place a second background square (square D) on top of square C, right side down; line up the raw edges all round and stitch the seam, stopping ¼in from the centre point (**i**).

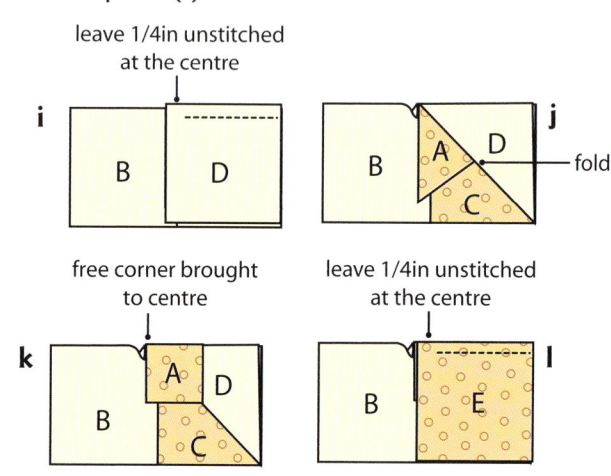

5 Fold square D diagonally (**j**); take the free corner of square A, and bring it to the centre point as shown (**k**), again making sure that the fabric point is tucked right into the centre of the shape. Take the final patterned square (square E) and place it wrong side up on the shape; line up the edges, and stitch the seam between square E and square D, stopping ¼in from the centre (**l**).

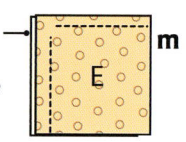

6 Finally, line up the edges and stitch the seam between square E and square B as shown; make sure that the raw edges of the folded square A are enclosed in this seam, and once again leave ¼in unstitched at the centre of the shape (**m**). Open up to reveal a Bow Tie (**n**)! On the back, press the seams around in a spiral as shown (**o**) to reduce bulk in the centre of the block.

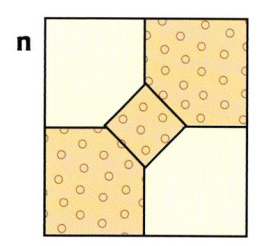

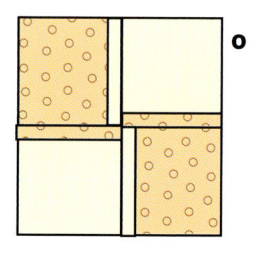

back of block

66

PROJECT 10

Bow Charming

Add a three-dimensional look to your quilt with interlocking circles of Bow Tie blocks.

Finished size: 50in (127cm) square
Charm pack featured: Birdie

You will need

- Two charm packs (containing a total of at least 81 5in squares)
- 80cm background fabric
- 30cm fabric for border 1
- 70cm fabric for border 2
- 40cm fabric for the binding
- 2.75m backing fabric
- Wadding, at least 54in square

Instructions

Use ¼in seams throughout

1 Cut each of the 81 charm squares into four 2½in squares – you will use three per Bow Tie, and keep one for the border. Cut 162 small squares from the background fabric, each measuring 2½in square.

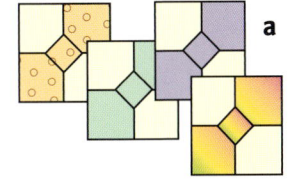

Follow the instructions on page 66 to make 81 Bow Tie blocks (**a**), each measuring 4½in square.

2 Arrange the blocks in nine rows of nine to create the pattern shown (**b**). Once you're happy with the arrangement, stitch the blocks into rows, and then join the rows to create the centre of the quilt top. Your design will now measure 36½in square.

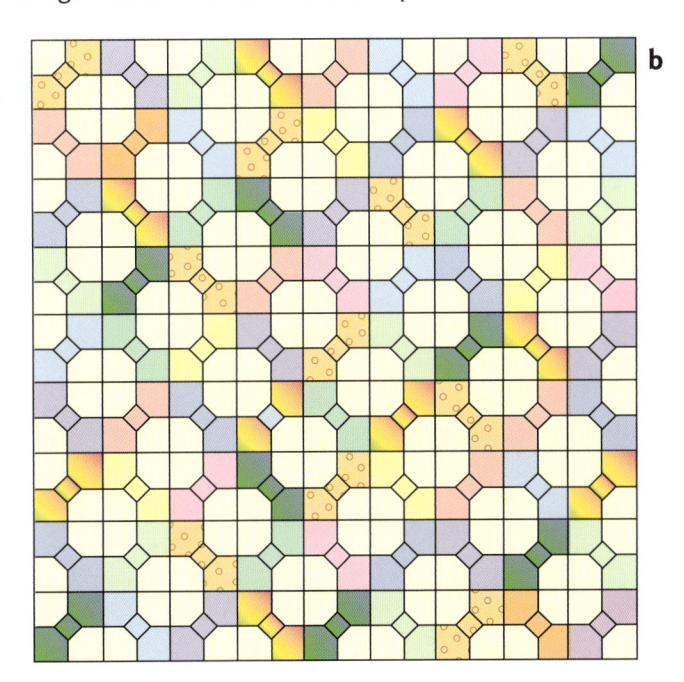

HINT
Press the seams open as you join the blocks and rows, to reduce the bulk in the seams.

PROJECT 10

c

3 From border 1 fabric cut four strips, each measuring 2½in x the width of the fabric. Trim two of these to 36½in and stitch them to the top and bottom of the quilt top; trim the other two to 40½in and sew to the sides (**c**).

4 From border 2 fabric cut five strips, each measuring 5in x the width of the fabric. Trim two of these to 40½in and stitch them to the top and bottom of the quilt top. Cut one of the remaining strips in half and join one half to each remaining border strip; trim these two new strips down to 50in and sew to the sides of the quilt (**d**).

Your quilt top is now complete; layer it with wadding and backing fabric, then quilt and bind as you wish.

HINT
Quilt a motif in each plain square created between the blocks; don't quilt over the Bow Ties themselves, or you will flatten them and lose their 3D effect.

d

The Bow Charming design in a different colourway

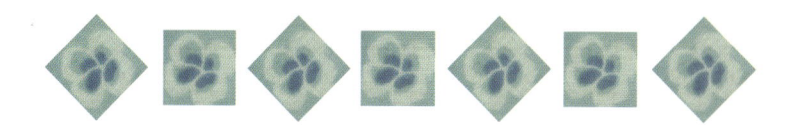

Acknowledgements and thanks to:

- Mimi Hollenbaugh for the Floating Flower Charms project
- Lesley, Judith, Mimi and Jenny – the fabulous staff at Puddleducks
- Andrew, Christopher and Alexandra – my wonderful family, who tolerate my obsession with fabric and patchwork!
- Sevenoaks Photography:
  48 Hollybush Lane, Sevenoaks TN13 3TL
  01732 742929 www.7oaksphotography.com
- Winbourne Fabrics – distributor of Moda fabrics in the UK: 01782 513380
- Gail and Chris Lawther – the editors and publishers; without their patience and expertise this book would not have happened
- Beryl Cadman at Custom Quilting Ltd, UK and European Distribution for Gammill Statler long-arm quilting machines

Kits for the projects in this book are available from Puddleducks, which also sells a wide range of Moda Charm Packs, fabrics and other quilting products.

**Puddleducks
116 St John's Hill
Sevenoaks
Kent TN13 3PD
tel 01732 743642
web www.puddleducksquilts.co.uk**

The quilts in this book were long-arm quilted at Puddleducks on a Gammill Statler Stitch machine.

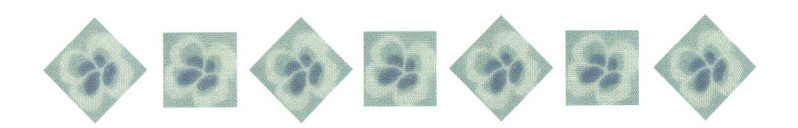

PUDDLEDUCKS
Long Arm Quilting Service

Many quilters love hand and domestic machine quilting. However, if you love the piecing but find the thought of quilting your project daunting, our long arm quilting service may provide the ideal solution.

Edge to edge quilting

We have a wide range of edge to edge patterns to complement your quilt pattern. Our prices include all the 100% cotton threads needed for the long arm quilting. You can see examples of available quilting patterns on the quilts in the shop and on the website; before we begin work we'll discuss your requirements and suitable patterns.

Wadding

We offer a choice of waddings to be used in your quilt. Please do not provide your own wadding, as if it has not been tested on the machine it may not give satisfactory results.

Backing fabric

Any of the 100% cotton fabrics on sale in the shop can be used as backing fabrics; we will advise the amount you need. We also have several extra-wide backing fabrics available. If you provide your own backing fabric please ensure that it is at least 4 inches bigger on all sides than the size of the quilt top.

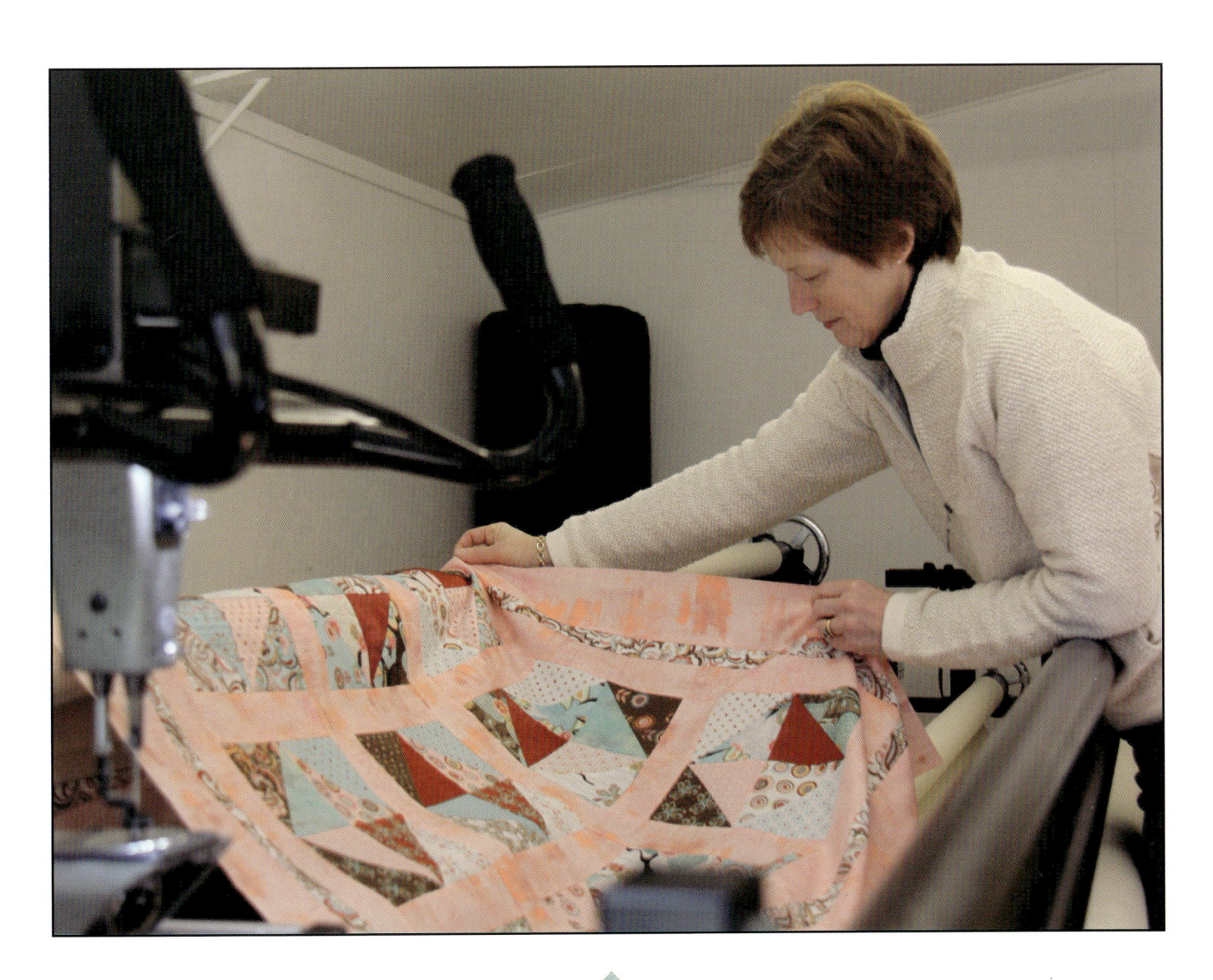

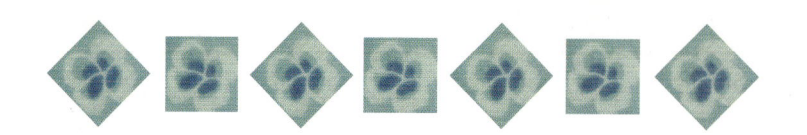

For your own notes ...